Acknowledgements

The origins of this book lie in the Student Transition and Retention (STAR) project (supported by the Fund for the Development of Teaching and Learning (Phase 4), Higher Education Funding Council for England and the Department of Higher & Further Education, Training and Employment, Northern Ireland), which examined the ways students might be better prepared for, and then cope with, their first year at university. We therefore thank the other members of the STAR project team for their enthusiastic discussion on all matters in relation to helping students in Higher Education. In alphabetical order these were Liz Gayton, Bill Norton, Helen Richardson and Steve Waite. Many other colleagues, too numerous to mention individually, provided valuable comments while this book was in conception, planning and draft stages, and we are grateful to them too.

Three other groups deserve special mention. Although we are teachers in Higher Education we are, perhaps more importantly, parents, and the contributions, both deliberate and unwitting, of our children have been vitally important. For these we thank Abigail, Andrew, Ian, Kathryn, Matthew and Richard. Our partners, Jennifer, Jill and Marylyn have made substantial sacrifices in order that this work was delivered on time and our gratitude goes to them. Finally, almost all we do in Higher Education is shaped by students; students from whom we have learned so much over the years. So we also thank the generations of students that we have had the privilege of helping, through education, to become mature, confident and independent individuals.

Mark Davies is Professor of Bioscience at the University of Sunderland

Tony Cook is Senior Lecturer and Director of the STAR project (*www.ulster.ac.uk/star*) at the University of Ulster

Brian S. Rushton is Reader in Biology at the University of Ulster

Contents

Chapter 1

Introduction – what this book is about

You the parent, Chris the student, and us the teachers

You are the parent of a teenager. This book is about you and how you can help your teenager who wants to study – or may already be studying – at university.

It doesn't matter whether you went to university or not: this book is still for you. If you did experience Higher Education – university-level education – that was probably long ago, but even if it wasn't, changes in Higher Education mean that your teenager's experience will be radically different from yours. Also, when you were younger, barely 15% of your age group went to university and now it seems like everybody's offspring is going.

UK Government statistics suggest that 43% of 18 year olds went into Higher Education in 2005 and this is set to rise to 50% by 2010. Consequently, this might be your family's first experience of going to university and you might be feeling a little in the dark as to what your teenager might experience.

In short, you are a typical parent of tomorrow's student. You know the importance of the coming decisions in a way that young people do not. You are faced with the problems of offering the best advice and support you can, but have a limited background. We and this book are here to help with that.

Chris, your aspiring teenager, is perhaps your eldest offspring and certainly wants to enter Higher Education in about two years' time – or may already be there. It does not matter whether Chris is male or female, but she is more likely to be female since 7% more women than men gained entrance to university in 2004/5. This is a trend that will probably continue.

Throughout this book we will use "Chris" as an example. She will be female throughout, but do not worry if you have a son. What is true of Chris, your daughter, will also be true of Chris, your son. Chris is apparently faced with a sequence of important life changing decisions. She will take them in her stride – kids that age do – without ever realising that each set of decisions opens one set of doors and closes another. She needs to decide what to do now, what choices to make before she enters university if she's not already there, and she needs to build realistic expectations of Higher Education. She will not be doing this alone since, whether you know it or not, you and others will guide her. But, of course, she is young and obviously knows what is best for her...

You will also find, throughout the book, specific examples, which we have called Case Studies, of real life situations which show how students we have known have dealt with the various problems and situations described in the book.

We are three teachers in Higher Education. We are probably, on average, a bit older than you are and some of our kids have been through the university system and emerged on the other side. And perhaps like Chris, our parents did not go to university either; our families had no history of Higher Education.

Chris may be joining our 'academic family' in two years' time or so. It is in our interests to ensure that Chris adopts us willingly and is not placed with us arbitrarily, that she will work with us, and that we are as proud of her when she graduates as you are now.

We have written this book to help you make sure that Chris makes sensible decisions about her future. We also want to make sure that neither you nor Chris get any unwelcome surprises in the next few years. But this is not a "follow our formula and you will succeed" book. Chris is in charge of her own success, or otherwise, and what is right for one student may be

2

completely wrong for another. Chris is an individual and you will know better than we do what might work for her and what might not.

We know from our own experiences that each student is unique. This is why there is no magic formula and we don't expect you, or Chris, to follow all our advice. Hence, for example, we supply advice on what to do if Chris finds herself on the "wrong" course, even though we spend time discussing how to choose a course so that the "wrong" ones can be avoided.

So this book is about you, the parents of students who are approaching or are in Higher Education in all its forms. That means mainly universities, but also includes those Higher Education courses outside universities, for example in Further Education Colleges. We've used "university" to mean any institution where Higher Education courses are taught, and "course" to mean a programme of study leading to an award such as a degree (for example B.A. or B.Sc.). The language of Higher Education can be confusing, even to us, so we have provided Chapter 13 *The jargon* at the end of this book, which we think you will find useful.

Getting into university – making reasoned choices
Why would Chris want to go to university at all? The publicity says that the likelihood of her getting a good job will be much greater with a degree than without, and it seems reasonable that this is true when so many of those already in the job market have degrees. And in any case what is the alternative? Leave school at 16 and try to get a job? But what job? With few paper qualifications there are few career opportunities. Staying on to do UK A levels, Scottish Highers or a vocational work-related qualification seems like a good idea, but what can you do with A

levels and similar qualifications that you can't do with GCSEs?

Chris needs help and that means that you need help. You have seen the circus on TV surrounding the A level results in the summer, with anxious students jostling for places. You have heard all about the good side of Higher Education: the job prospects; the increased lifetime earning potential; and the social life – but there is a down side as well. How can you avoid the problems? Problems like getting a place – how can you avoid the late summer scramble to get Chris on to an appropriate course?

Chris is probably now looking at what qualifications she will need to enter Higher Education on the course she wants to study. This is not too soon to discuss her long-term aspirations. The UK GCSE results and teachers' advice might lead you to believe that continuing in her best subjects (for example History, Biology and Geography) would maximise her results and therefore her chances of getting a place at a 'good' university. This might be true, but is no good if she wants to specialise at university in a subject for which these are not a suitable preparation.

It may seem to be too early to be deciding on a career, but now is the time to start taking the long view. What is her best route to the career she wants to pursue, UK A levels or Scottish Highers, vocational A levels, or other forms of entrance qualifications? What are her preferred career paths and perhaps, just as important, what are not? She does not want to start unnecessarily closing doors, but the path she chooses now will determine what opportunities are immediately available.

Universities and courses vary in their attitude to entry qualifications. Some expect to have students with a prescribed combination of qualifications at high grades for particular degrees; others are more flexible. Courses vary in the intake grades and qualifications required for entry. What does this mean? Are those with higher intake grades better or just more popular? Or maybe they are trying to filter out students who might take more effort to teach with the implication that the teaching may not be as good. Anyone can make a silk purse out of a piece of silk. Should Chris apply to those institutions that are offering to take her with her highest predicted grades on the assumption that these must be the "best" places in which to learn?

Choices made about the course and the institution will have a profound influence on Chris's future and to some extent those choices are being made from age 13 in the UK when choices about subjects to study for GCSEs or their Scottish equivalents are made. You, of course, will never know what the alternative futures would have been had you made different choices. When choosing courses and institutions, therefore, encourage Chris to make informed and positive choices and not to look back.

No matter what choices are made now or in the future, remember that no avenue is ever really closed; the journey might just be a little longer. This is the era of life long learning during which few can expect to have a single lifetime career and most will undergo retraining between, or even within, jobs. We had a colleague at university who initially studied history and then he decided he wanted to do medicine. It took time and, obviously, money, but he got there in the end.

One of our own sons went to university to study Chemistry and four years later ended up with a degree in Computer Science. He was never forced through failure to change direction but made a series of sensible decisions for him. All his parents ever did was to listen to his arguments and help him to refine them until he knew that those arguments made sense, and his parents validated his decisions with unequivocal approval.

In Chapters 2 and 3 (*Student timeline*) we will take you through the steps that you will take between now and when Chris gets her first job. When will you and Chris be taking life-changing decisions? Which decisions matter and which do not? Who is going to help you; who are the experts? Who has a vested interest in the decisions Chris might make and who is most likely to have her best interests at heart? Whose advice can you trust? And perhaps most importantly, how to choose a course and a university.

Getting the study right

Success at university is as much about commitment as it is about intellect. Commitment does not only equate to hard work. It is also about joining in, attending not only the timetabled sessions but forming and contributing to what we call learning communities (small groups of students who work together); joining in the life on the campus and developing networks of mutually supportive friends and colleagues. Being a student is much more than going to lectures and doing the work.

When Chris is at university she will be doing things that you never had the opportunity to do. She will start asking questions and seeking advice about things you may know nothing about. What are you going to say when she asks for advice about joining the Dead Parrot Society? How can you offer sympathetic counsel when you may not understand? What are you going to say when she asks you nothing at all and keeps her university life screened off from you? Chapter 4 (*What it's like at university*) will help you to appreciate Chris's university experience and help you to give good advice.

You may have gained the impression that at university Chris will be sitting around in lecture theatres listening to old men droning on about things

6

that no one else understands. This may not appear to be what Chris should be doing in two or three years' time! And what about the exams? The GCSEs were bad enough. So much riding on so little. And the coursework.

At least at school there was a lot of help from the teachers but what can Chris expect at university and how can you support her? How can you and Chris develop reasonable expectations of life at university so that you can make reasonable decisions and not be disappointed? We want to set your mind at rest and to do that you need information about the work she will be doing at university. Chapters 5, 6 and 7 will tell you about *Learning, Assessment* and *Teaching* at university. The more prepared you are, the better equipped you will be to offer sound advice.

Chapter 5 is about *Learning*. Some students come to university with an expectation that they will be taught everything they need to know. This assumes that teaching staff know everything and that everything is known. But most university staff will have a strong background in research, and research is really about questioning things. That means that we do NOT know. New students often come from systems with a defined syllabus in which everything that candidates need to know and should be able to do is written down and tested. The idea that Chris will at some stage be expected to find out something that her teachers do not know can be a strange one. Furthermore, university staff make compromises. They make decisions about how much time to spend doing different aspects of their jobs. Some will be doing mainly research and will be rarely accessible to students while others will give their teaching a higher priority. Learning at university then is about organisation, collaboration and independence.

Chapter 6 is about *Assessment*. Universities are assessing institutions. We are authorised to assess the abilities of our students and universities award degrees, diplomas and certificates on the basis of our judgements. It is an awesome responsibility. Students can teach themselves, they can and do learn by themselves but they cannot assess themselves and award themselves degrees. We know that different students learn in different ways and so our assessment systems are very varied. Chris will like some forms of assessment and not others. She will probably think that some of it is unfair. You and she need to know how we run our assessment systems so that you know what is happening and what is important and what is not.

Chapter 7 will tell you about our *Teaching*; or rather, how we encourage students to learn. The transition from being a supported learner to being an independent one occurs gradually between year one at university and graduation, and then through into employment. We design our teaching that way. At school, Chris will have a close network of friends and teachers who have known her for many years. When she eventually leaves she will be at the top of the school both socially and academically. Her teachers will probably have been setting her work that has to be completed to a strict timetable with short deadlines.

Her teachers will go through every word and may even help her re-write some of it for formal assessment. When she enters university she will start as a stranger, maybe in classes of 200 or more. Depending on the subject she studies there may be relatively few hours timetabled in the classroom and she may feel that the rest of the time is her own. How are you going to advise her when she spends Friday to Monday at home because all her classes are on Tuesday and Thursday? She will be set work with long deadlines and will be expected to manage her own time. University staff will make this change to independent learning as gentle as they can, but she will have to develop new learning strategies to cope effectively. She may seek your advice and approval. What are you going to tell her?

Getting help

Most students will be like Chris when she goes to university and will therefore be between the ages of 17 and 21. What were you like at 18? Were you well-grounded, sensible, logical and mature? Well, the chances are, Chris is not going to be either. Mistakes will be inevitable, but a university is a safe environment in which to make them. Just because you will not be there all the time, however, does not mean there will be no support. There will be professional help with academic development and with health and social issues. Your role as a parent will still be important.

As academic staff we will impose high expectations on Chris and eventually demand work of the highest quality. But we know that Chris is not the finished article on arrival and our teaching and support are designed to suit the academic and social development that students go through during the three years of the typical degree course. Chris has little need for the burden of parental expectation as well. So she will need your unequivocal support through what might be difficult but also exciting times. There will be high spots and low spots, excitement and disappointment, approval and disapproval, mistakes and triumphs; but the comfort of a stable, supportive and undemanding family background will help Chris through.

Universities are relatively self-contained and Chris can expect to find all the support she needs on campus, so in Chapter 8 (*Student support services*) we will tell you about the helpful services Chris can expect to find in a typical university. This will reassure you that facilities will be available, but Chris will have to go and get the help herself. University staff rarely go out searching for problems to solve so we are reliant on Chris's good sense to seek the help she needs.

Getting money

We do not know how much money Chris will owe when that first job comes along, especially since we do not yet know when her university career will start, much less finish. The debt, however, will probably be considerable but at least it will not be yours – unless you choose it to be. Students are no longer considered to be solely dependent on their parents for financial support. They are old enough to have credit cards and personal accounts and they are old enough to take the responsibility of a debt. Her debt will not grow as fast as yours would have done over the same period because interest rates for students are pegged to the rate of inflation.

The debt is balanced by the prospect of a higher income when she enters a graduate profession and does not have to be repaid until a threshold income is reached. Chris can also work while at university. Indeed more than money can be gained by the experience of work at this time. In addition, she may choose to complete not only a first degree but may need some further qualification in order to practise in a chosen profession – or she might just enjoy studying at university level.

At least one of us continued into study at a postgraduate level simply because we loved the subject with little consideration of where the money might come from. With hindsight, better planning and earlier decision-making might have been appropriate and would certainly have lessened the financial burden.

So there are choices to make – how long to spend at university, how much is it reasonable to borrow, how much time is it reasonable to spend in paid or unpaid employment, how to manage that crucial balance between working, studying and socialising? Chris will tackle these decisions one at a time and in the light of conditions at the time. To help her make the right decisions you will need to know the sorts of things to advise Chris to consider.

In Chapter 9 (*Money*) we will discuss with you the financial side of a university career. We, however, are not financial advisors. Student finance is dependent on the vagaries of a government policy that can change rapidly. We will not be able to predict how things will be when Chris is at university. What is certain, however, is that she will be faced with the same decisions that all students have to make, to work or not to work, where to get extra cash, and whether to go for a higher qualification or not. You still want to know how much, don't you? Well, a survey by a high street bank revealed that in 2006 the average graduate debt was just over £13,000, but remember that this is only an average and that with good planning Chris's debt is likely to be considerably less.

Even so, if you now think there's no point in reading on, consider the financial *benefits*. A survey in 2005 by a team at Swansea University found that graduates will earn on average about £150,000 more over a lifetime than those with just A levels. In some subjects the difference could be in excess of £225,000. A similar study in 2007 by Universities UK, which provides a voice for all the UK's universities, reported these figures as £160,000 and £340,000, respectively. So don't worry… yet!

Getting out of university – early

It sounds from the year-on-year publicity that new, dissatisfied students are leaving university in droves. What do those figures actually mean? Chris may decide that she has made a mistake and wants to leave her course. Is dropping out such a bad thing? What are the consequences for her and others?

About 10% of students do not complete the course on which they started. Some of these students actually change institution. Only about 8% drop out of Higher Education entirely. Many who leave university do so in the first few weeks. They very rapidly come to the decision that they have made a mistake and they solve the problem by leaving. What do they learn in those first few weeks and how can you have access to that information earlier to help Chris make better decisions? Is dropping out the end of her academic career?

In chapter 10 (*Avoiding and recovering from a poor start*) we will discuss the events that might lead up to Chris dropping out and what the consequences will be if she does decide to leave the course. We will advise how you can help her to make the best of a less than sparkling performance *before* dropping out is inevitable.

Getting away from the nest

One day Chris is going to live away from home, cook for herself, do her own washing, and may bring up your grandchildren. One day Chris will be independent not only of you but also of the teachers who have worked in the schools and universities she has attended.

The transition from dependent living to independent living can be much more sudden than the academic changes. Many students leave the bosom of their families for the very first time when they go to university. We have had complaints from students on a field trip in the first week of the first year because they were unable to get a clear mobile phone signal. This was the first time they had been away from family support.

So, is it best to live at home while at university and postpone independence day? Or is it best to be a resident student and start independent living and studying all at the same time? Should you allow this to influence Chris's choice of university? And whose best interest have you in mind when you discuss with Chris whether she applies to the nearest university and lives at home to study, or goes further afield?

The performance of a university tends not to be judged so much by the qualifications gained by its graduates as by their employability and reputation in the wider world. We could coddle our students so that they all would do extremely well in their examinations. After all, we do the teaching and set and mark all the assessments. It would not be difficult to ensure most students performed well in these tests. But when we are measured by a different sort of outcome and have different sorts of aspirations for our students, we behave in a different sort of way: one that promotes student independence.

You and we share a common objective, one that Chris will not be aware of yet. We want her to be independent; to enter the world of work as a freethinking, well-motivated individual who knows what she is capable of and when to seek help. In Chapter 11 (*What next?*) we will describe how job hunting is supported in universities and what employers will be looking for, and consider other options after university. We have left this until last because it will bring together many of the aspects of learning, assessment and what university is like. This should allow you to make sense – see the purpose, if you like – of what Chris and we have been doing during her time at university.

Opening a dialogue ...

The person we really want to help is Chris. If she's 16, the two years studying for UK A levels, Scottish Highers or their equivalent might seem like a long time to her, let alone the five years it may be until she graduates. To her that five years is a third of a lifetime. Chris needs our help to plan for the long term but we have not met her yet and she is not going to read this book.

The best person, the most powerful person, we can talk to at the moment is you, her parent. Armed with the right questions and access to appropriate information you can help her plot a course through the approaching minefield. But we are not blinkered idealists. We know only too well how difficult it is to talk to young adults who also happen to be our children. It's important to establish a sympathetic and listening approach, so that you can help when she needs advice. It would be great for us to be able to say, "Now open, and keep open, a dialogue with Chris about her plans and experiences regarding Higher Education." If you're able to do this, then that's wonderful. For most of us the reality will be somewhat different. Expect your powers of persuasion to be tested!

Chapter 2

Student timeline: before university

In both this chapter and the next one we want to take you through the steps a typical student – as if there were such a person – takes during university education, and highlight those critical points where you can have a positive impact and what that impact might be. The steps start long before Chris enters university and finish long afterwards, as you will see.

The UK education system consists of two parts. There is a compulsory part that Chris has probably just completed and there is an optional part on which Chris is now probably embarking. Chris's experiences in compulsory education will be different in almost all respects from those in the optional part. Compulsory education occurs up to the age of 16 and is driven chronologically.

By this we mean that up until now Chris has moved from class to class because she has been getting older, not because she has achieved a standard of work indicating that she is ready to do the work in the next year. In the optional part, Chris will only advance on merit. Within reason, she can go as fast or as slow as suits her and if those teaching her feel she needs to go back and do something again then that is what she will be recommended to do. This flexibility also means that she will have to make choices and take the initiative in moving through the system, though to begin with she might need a little help from you.

To get into university she will require some entry qualifications. Which ones she needs are determined by the course she eventually wants to do and the universities at which she might want to do it. So choices made now about what qualifications she will have when she applies to university will determine which doors are open and which are closed at that point in time.

The same is true all the way along the timeline: decisions made now affect the ones Chris will be able to make in the future. That even sounds scary to us! But don't worry – there are many, many doors and very few close completely, as we will explain a little later. The purpose of this chapter and the next, which both concern the student timeline, is therefore to warn you when choices will happen and how important they might be, so you can offer advice at the right moment.

Predicting critical events

A few lines ago we expressed doubt about there being a 'typical student', so instead of generalising we'll supply an example. It's the first of a series of Case Studies in this book and may help you to identify critical events in Chris's transit through the education system.

CASE STUDY – JOSHUA

Joshua was outgoing and bright but not very sensible. He had difficulty in concentrating on anything for any length of time. He laughed his way through secondary school and had a really good time. He conned his father into making his technology project in the garage, although he did manage to design it himself. He took a standard set of GCSEs at the local comprehensive school in 2000 and got BBCCDDE.

This was good enough for him to progress to a sixth form college to study A levels, but he decided that he had had enough of school and opted to go to a further education college and take a BTEC (Business and Technology Education Council) qualification in Land Administration. He chose this subject because a pal of his was going to do it at the same time and because he envied the flashy company cars of estate agents.

Joshua found that Land Administration was not what he thought it might be, largely because he didn't read the promotional material for the course, and detested the module on Law. He realised he had made a poor choice of course and, by December 2000, he was close to leaving but persisted, largely because his elder brother sat down with him and talked through what his options would be if he dropped out.

He fell in with a group of computer games players at college and decided that designing computer games was the career for him. So he applied to five universities through the Universities and Colleges Admissions Service (UCAS) in the autumn of 2001 to study Computer Games Design. Some of his choices rejected his application outright, probably deeming that his qualifications were not appropriate.

With better research Joshua could have predicted this: he could have visited his prospective universities to discuss his options. Eventually, though, one university, just one, offered him the chance of a place on an Honours degree course: a four-year course at a Scottish university.

Joshua gained the grades in Land Administration that he needed for entry and heard that he had a place. In September 2002 he packed his games console, a TV, a few clothes (mainly in black) and was driven by his parents to university. Joshua was much more focused in his first year at university than he had been at college. He had to catch up on aspects of maths and computing, about which he knew nothing. The facts that his university-owned accommodation was in the centre of town and that he had a rather unruly and work-shy set of flatmates did not help. He tried to move out but could only do so if he could find someone else to take his place in the flat. He had to stick it out, and the combination of an active social life at night and the new subjects he was meeting during the day hampered his progress. He failed two modules in the May/June examinations but managed to pass them when he re-sat them in September 2003.

Joshua progressed to year two, but his confidence was severely dented and he hadn't written any games yet! Studying was still difficult. When he was at the further education college, the staff seemed to know when he was having trouble and had helped him through the bad patches. At university the staff only knew he was having problems if he told them or if he failed something. He was not having the great time that he had expected and moved out of university accommodation into a flat near the campus which he shared with a fellow student.

In 2004, before the beginning of his third year, Joshua took a six-month work placement during which he was involved in designing web pages and visiting clients to discuss their needs. This was the first time he had had a real job and taken on real responsibilities. He found the experience stimulating and looked forward to the day when he would enter the job market and do something interesting full-time. The placement extended his course by six months.

In his third year Joshua worked hard but felt he needed to get a job so he decided to leave at the end of that year rather than stay the extra year it would have taken him to get an Honours degree. He duly completed his third year, and left university in early 2006 having been awarded an 'Ordinary' degree. He applied for jobs in web design but in the meantime took a job in data entry in an insurance company just to earn some money.

By mid 2007 Joshua had not found a job as a web designer but had stayed with the insurance company, where he quickly progressed into project management. His managers saw a potential in him that even he did not know was there and put him on a series of training courses. He was no longer in computing, nor for that matter in Land Administration. But the experience he gained on those courses equipped him well to perform the sorts of tasks that his employers expected of him: he gained people skills, organisation skills, and, above all, coping skills.

So where did the choices really come in this brief life history? Where would different choices have made radical changes to the outcome? We, of course, cannot tell for sure but Joshua:

- chose a course at an FE college;
- chose to go directly to university and not take a gap year;
- chose a degree course and a university;
- chose to do a placement; and finally
- chose a profession, or rather it chose him.

These were all critical choices. None of them turned out for Joshua in a predictable way, but had he chosen differently, alternative futures could have opened up for him.

So what's the point of all this for you, Chris's parent? First, Joshua stuck at it. When he found Land Administration was not to his liking he stuck it out and used that qualification to move onto something he liked better. When he had trouble in his first year, again he stuck at it and things did indeed get better. Often persisting with a course until a suitable exit point is found is much better than just throwing in the towel. Chris should use the experiences she has gained as a springboard to her next experience and you might have to make her aware of this.

Second, although Joshua's parents were influential, the support from a sibling was even more important. If Chris isn't naturally receptive to your suggestions – few teenagers are – who can you use as an intermediary?

Third, he did a placement. Experience of work was critical in motivating Joshua and changed his whole approach to work. It is likely that his choice of course was critical, not because the subject material was important but because the discipline of computing and its associated work developed his management skills. His placement showed him that he could work well with people. Would a placement suit Chris?

Fourth and finally, doors did not close for Joshua just because he made a sequence of poor decisions. He chose a BTEC rather than A levels and this may have reduced the number of universities he could have applied to. On the other hand he showed some success in the more open atmosphere of a further education college where he might have failed entirely at a sixth form college or school. He opted for courses that, as it turned out, were unrelated to his eventual career.

But, by completing the courses, he learned much about himself and about working, and it was these qualities that got him into a job in the end. The overriding lesson, however, is that doors do not close; they stay open. It is only the timing of when students can get through them that changes.

In the rest of the timeline we describe a sequence of events. The sequence is the shortest possible. Poor decisions need not change it, they only make it longer, which may not be a bad thing. It certainly wasn't for Joshua.

Entry qualifications

The first critical decision is about the choice of qualifications Chris should take in order to get into university. She knows what she has been successful at; her GCSE (or equivalent) results will show her that. Has she made a career choice yet? If she already knows what she wants to do for the rest of her life then *Bravo!* She's one of the lucky ones and you should point her to a careers advisor to discuss the optimum route to that outcome. Advice will be plentiful and accurate for those who know precisely what they want. But 16 is a tender age for students to have mapped out their future.

Most students do not know how they want their lives to develop when they graduate, let alone when they choose their entry qualifications. Further, at 16 they're often not even remotely interested in finding out about planning for the future. This is neither a disaster nor unusual; but Chris does need to make sensible choices now to make things easier later on. Convincing her of this might be difficult, but persevere, because it will bring its own rewards.

Get hold of a few university prospectuses either at your local library or on-line (just type a university name followed by *.ac.uk* into a search engine and you will get to its home page). There is normally a link direct to the prospectus from a university's home page. Read about the types of courses on offer: often course content is very different from what you'd imagine. Discuss with Chris the entry qualifications and if she's likely to achieve them.

Although Chris may not know precisely what she wants to do, she will almost certainly have a general idea of the areas in which she feels comfortable working. She will need to make a decision about whether she wants to study in an area which is likely to have specific subject requirements, in which case her choice of subjects as entry qualifications is important. Think about the notion of studying a combination of subjects that will allow admittance to a wide range of courses. At least that way Chris can put off making narrowing decisions until she has to apply to universities.

If she is leaning towards degree courses that have less specific requirements, then she needs to choose subjects that will both be useful and will maximise her "UCAS points". The Universities and Colleges Admissions Service (UCAS) handles the admissions process on behalf of universities. There is a complex arrangement whereby entry qualifications, such as A levels and Scottish Highers, attract points (tariff points) and for many courses at many universities a certain number of points is required for entry.

Check the UCAS website (*www.ucas.com*), or ask a careers advisor for more details. UCAS has on its website the Stamford Test (*www.ucas.com/stamford*). This asks questions about what a prospective student would like to do and about his or her attributes. It then gives a list of potential courses that fit the student's profile. This is an extremely blunt instrument but as a starting point it will help you to discuss with Chris her course options and will help limit the number of courses you and Chris need to consider.

But if Chris knows what she wants to do and is prepared to work for it, then it is worth persisting. One of our sons chose to take A level Mathematics without having first taken Additional Mathematics at GCSE. This was against the advice of the sixth form college. At the end of the first year of the course he was not doing well, largely because much of the course expected knowledge that the Additional Mathematics would have given him.

He was advised to change to Religious Knowledge which was thought to be easier and to guarantee better grades. Against advice he persisted with Mathematics and, on more familiar ground in year two and with some additional support, eventually got a grade A in Maths, much to the college's surprise. This story should not encourage you to ignore advice; it is well meant. But sometimes perseverance can win out if students are determined enough.

Also consider that many university subjects have an area of study within them that students find difficult. In Biology this is Chemistry, in Psychology it is Statistics, in Engineering it is Mathematics. The difficulty may arise because university teachers are so specialised that they find it hard to teach at a level that is appropriate for those with no experience of the subject at all. It can be important therefore, that appropriate combinations of entry qualifications are taken, at least at AS level or equivalent.

In choosing entry qualifications it is not always the best choice to follow Chris's best subjects at GCSE. This can lead to bizarre combinations of subjects that may not match the entry requirements for any particular degree programme. Biology, Religious Education and Music might well maximise a particular student's UCAS points score, but it is a poor preparation for many degrees. It would be acceptable for a Business Management degree, but would it be a good preparation?

Implicit in the above is our concentration on conventional UK A levels. Although the A level route is the most popular into university, it is by no means the only one. Some, such as the International Baccalaureate Diploma, have a similar balance of coursework and exams to A levels but many others are dominated by coursework that can be completed in a student's own time, often in subjects in which students have prior experience or interests. Vocational

A levels, for example, are increasingly popular. They combine academic study with experience of the work place. Some students can do exceptionally well at such qualifications, especially those who do not perform well in examinations. Universities, however, have been slow to adjust to students who enter with little recent experience of sitting examinations. In the two years Chris spends preparing portfolios for a vocational qualification she might well lose the skills, examination technique for example, which helped her achieve her grades at GCSE level.

Vocational qualifications are an excellent preparation for some university courses, but be careful to match the sort of work done, prior to entry, to that Chris might expect to have to do immediately on entry. It is therefore worth investigating early the nature of the course she might be applying for in two years' time.

Taking a gap year

Our message is to encourage Chris not to go straight to university from school. She should take a year out provided she does something useful with it. If Chris chooses not to take a year out she will probably be about 21 when she graduates. She will graduate enthused with ideas about what she wants to do and with a debt that she will want to pay off. She will most probably go straight into work or further study.

Between school and university is a good time, possibly the only time, to build up reserves without the pressures and responsibilities that she will have later. She can build up reserves of money and minimise her later debt, she can build up a reserve of skills that will be useful in her course and, if she can get a job related to her future course, she can build up a reserve of knowledge. Most of all, however, she can gain experience of the realities of life outside an educational institution, and these realities may well spur her on to succeed at university.

The gap year is probably the best time to start building an attractive CV (Curriculum Vitae – see Chapter 11 *What next?*) that will serve her well throughout her university career and guide her into employment later. For many, 'gap year' means travelling. This is undoubtedly a good 'broadening' experience too and could mature Chris quite rapidly. It might mature you too as you wonder what she's up to in Hong Kong or wherever! Searching the web for advice is a good start. Try sites like:

www.gap-year.com
www.findastudentjob.com   and
www.findagap.com.

Only you are in the position to tell her that taking a year off to do her own thing may be near impossible later in her life, especially if she has a full-time job or children.

Starting the application process

Most courses that give qualifications for university entrance, such as A levels or Scottish Highers, last two academic years. Typically Chris will apply for university, a process managed by UCAS, at the start of the second year. Both you and Chris should consult the UCAS website extensively. Its information will be up-to-date and available as you need it. UCAS, schools, colleges and careers advisors can describe the process in detail, so we just want to make sure you are prepared by giving you the bare bones – to inform you of when you might like to offer support.

Most students apply *before* they know what grades they have gained. Students can apply for up to five courses (five is the UCAS maximum). University admissions officers will make preliminary decisions on the basis of the subject mix Chris is studying, the grades predicted by her teachers, her personal statement, and the opinions of her teachers.

She may be invited for an interview – this will depend on the policy of the university and the course. Chris may then receive a conditional offer, i.e. she will only gain admittance if she gains specific grades in her forthcoming examinations. Then Chris will have to decide which offers she wants to accept.

Chris could, however, apply *after* she has gained the qualifications she needs for entry. In this case she should visit her target institutions and courses, discuss whether her qualifications are appropriate and only apply to those five courses from which she gets a positive response. She will most likely receive "unconditional offers" from these institutions and will have the opportunity of accepting just one.

The details of the timing of events obviously vary every year and universities respond to applications with varying speed. It is therefore difficult to predict key dates with any accuracy. A rough guide, however, is that if you meet a mid-January deadline for application through UCAS then you can expect all offers to be made by early May at the latest.

There is a late application scheme, the deadline for which is in late June. Applications received by this deadline will be responded to by mid-July. Whenever the application is received by UCAS the response to Chris will state a date by which a decision about acceptance or rejection has to be made by her chosen universities.

Choosing a course and open days

Chris will probably want to do an Honours degree. This typically takes 4 years of full-time study in Scotland and 3 years in the rest of the UK. But bearing Joshua in mind, the Honours degree isn't the only exit point. Students can leave university with other, lesser, qualifications too, such as Certificates and Diplomas in Higher Education and Ordinary degrees.

Check out exactly what's on offer. Qualifications aren't always as straightforward as you might think. For example, in the UK students who complete a course in Medicine are typically, but not always, awarded two degrees, one in medicine and one in surgery. Both are Ordinary degrees. Likewise so-called "undergraduate Masters" are becoming more popular, where students study for 4 years and emerge with a Masters degree. It's complex. Make sure you and Chris check it out.

Chris needs to find out as much as she can about the subjects she wants to study at university and where she would most like to study them. Draw on as many sources of information as possible. Look back through her school reports. Is she as good/bad as you think she is? Where are her strengths, what grades is she likely to get in the summer? What has the Stamford Test told you about her preferred subject areas?

Remember that no two university courses are the same. Even ones with the same titles can be radically different at different universities. This is in part because courses are often driven by the research expertise of staff and where the expertise differs, the courses differ. For example, if Chris wants to specialise in International Law, she should choose an Honours degree in Law course where there is a large element of international law, rather than just a single module. Again, find out early!

As far as admissions are concerned we can classify courses into three types and it is worth thinking about which type Chris is applying for.

"Selecting courses" expect a large number of well-qualified applicants. Their admissions procedures are devoted to reducing the numbers of students admitted to a manageable number, so they pick from the best applicants. Selecting courses tend to be in the universities with strong research reputations. They also include professional courses in many of the others. This is because the professions engage in "manpower planning" by limiting the intake to those numbers that could reasonably be expected to get professional jobs after they graduate.

Medicine and the health related professions, such as Pharmacy, are obvious examples of such courses which do not often enter UCAS's "clearing" system, more about which later, which matches unplaced students to unfilled courses. You may find that some selecting courses, for example, *some* Medicine and *some* Law courses, ask applicants to sit a selection examination which can be used to discriminate between applicants on grounds other than their formal qualifications.

"Recruiting courses" struggle every year to fill their places. They actively recruit for students. After the A level results are published they will drop their asking grades until they fill their places. Applicants who cannot get places on the selecting courses may get offers from universities to join recruiting courses. These courses tend not to be linked directly to a profession, so their graduates will be found in an extremely wide variety of roles and opting for a recruiting course may allow Chris to defer her choice of ultimate career.

"Sink courses" are extremely popular. They have no problem filling their quota of students even when other courses are unable to fill theirs. Sink courses are used by universities to top up their numbers to counter the shortfall elsewhere. They tend to have large class sizes and be non-professional courses where manpower planning is not an issue. These courses will have places available in "clearing".

Selecting courses will be difficult to get into and will require high grades. If she gets a place, Chris will probably be well-taught but in relatively large classes. She will be among other well-qualified students and be part of a high-performing community of students. A recruiting course, on the other hand, will contain a mixture of students; some will be highly qualified and highly committed to the subject, others will be less so. Class sizes could be smaller and she might get more individual treatment.

A sink course could have a very large number of students indeed and again have students with a variety of appropriate and not so appropriate qualifications. Joshua in the case study joined a sink course. Irrespective of how gifted Chris may be, it is worth choosing a few selecting courses and a few recruiting courses to apply to.

This is so that if she does well in her entry qualifications she will get into the selecting course, and if she does less well she can fall back on the recruiting course. Of course she needs to be sensible and select courses all of which she could see herself doing, all leading in roughly the direction she would like to go and all in universities and towns that she has visited.

University staff will not tell you whether they run a selecting, recruiting or a sink course. And you cannot tell from the subject. What will be recruiting at one university may well be sink at another. You will need to read between the lines. Go to an open day or be brazen and telephone: ask whether the course entered clearing last year; ask what the actual intake grade profile was compared to the asking grades; and ask whether the course carries recognition by, or is accredited by, a professional body.

Many courses will invite applicants either for interview or for a visit. This is a valuable opportunity to look around a campus and get a feel for it. Chris must go! If she's doubtful, you must persuade her. We cannot stress this strongly enough. Many a student has dropped out of university because of issues concerning the university or its location that could so easily have been spotted on a visit. Chris must go!

The purpose of visits or interviews is two-fold. First, if Chris performs very well in the interview this may encourage the university to make a lower offer. Remember that the asking grades may merely be a means of controlling numbers, not necessarily an indication of the talents required to complete the course. Second, an interview will enable Chris to find out more about the course and university. Interviews are often accompanied by a tour of the departmental facilities and existing students often lead these tours.

So don't take the university's word for what it has to say about itself. Talk to these students and pump them for information! This is a unique opportunity for Chris to find out what the course and the university are *really* like from a student's perspective. If an interview or visit/open day is optional, then take it. Go with Chris if you can. Universities are aware of the worries – not to mention financial obligations – of parents and so typically welcome them. In fact the presence of parents at these events is becoming the norm and most prospective students don't seem to mind bringing their parents with them.

The most thoughtful universities will separate you from Chris early in the tour and treat parents and other family members differently. You will have the opportunity to ask the questions you want, while Chris will be finding out what she wants to know. These are not necessarily the same.

You should be finding out about finances, class sizes and teaching methods. But if you're already clued up on what's on offer, join Chris for the tour of the teaching or social facilities. Ask questions about early leaving rates. Most students who leave early do so because they are disappointed with the course or university: it has not met the expectations that the university may have worked hard to build up during the application process. Failure rates are a different matter.

Students often fail because they have not organised their time properly, because they have been encouraged only to think in terms of passing, and because they have yet to come to terms with the differences between the expectations of university and of school.

So ask specifically about early leaving rates and failure rates in the course. Chris should be able to ensure she doesn't fail, but she can't control the university's presentation of itself.

Also make sure you get a chance to wander around without a guide – soak up the atmosphere and try to imagine what studying and/or living there would be like. Make sure you go in term-time when the university won't be slumbering. The visit or open day or interview offers a chance for you and Chris to discuss a prospective university from first-hand experience.

It will be difficult trying to persuade Chris that the course at University X is more suited to her needs than that at University Y if Chris has visited them but you haven't. It will be worthwhile engaging Chris in a discussion of the merits and drawbacks of prospective universities following a visit – at least to get Chris thinking about the factors she ought to take into consideration in making a final choice.

Finally in this section, a warning. It is Chris who has to spend three or so years studying a course at a university – not you. Support, support, support and gently persuade if you must, but never pressurise Chris into studying a particular subject or going to a particular university. And be careful here, you may not know that you are applying pressure.

Ask Chris if she is applying to the courses and universities *she* wants to and recognise that she might not be willing to tell you that she feels the pressure.

Students who make choices based on the expectations of others quickly become demoralised at university, often make much less than a perfect start and are home for good by Christmas.

Choosing a university and what the league tables really mean

League tables, often sponsored and published by national newspapers, will give you some indication of where universities sit relative to others.

League tables are based on measurements of relatively few aspects of a university and often these may not apply in detail to the courses you and Chris are interested in.

Treat league tables with caution. Focus on the teaching measures and select only those measures that are important to you. Let's take a number of measures of university performance and see how individual institutions compare.

Because these tables change from year-to-year it is unfair to specify an individual university, so let's imagine the first one is called Fleming University. This is a middle-size institution with a full range of subjects. It is a "pre-1992" institution. That is to say it was a university before 1992 and not one of the polytechnics and other colleges that were given university status in that or subsequent years. It has a strong reputation for progressive liberal education.

The second is Darwin University. It is a former polytechnic situated in an industrial city. It has a reputation for taking in students with a wide variety of backgrounds and for treating them well. It has an emphasis towards vocational courses.

Our third institution, Pasteur University, is a very large well-established institution in a large and cosmopolitan city.

The numbers in the table below are the three universities' ranking positions in a variety of measures related to their teaching. For any measure, the university with the greatest score is placed first in the ranking, the university with the second greatest score is placed second in the ranking, etc. The university scoring the least is placed 114th, since there are 114 universities in our imaginary system.

Measure	Fleming	Darwin	Pasteur
Qualifications of students entering	47	109	36
Staff to student ratio	46	100	28
Student satisfaction	41	61	16
Proportion of students who complete their studies	31	103	29
Proportion of students entering graduate jobs	48	103	77
Proportion of students leaving with good Honours degrees	88	76	34
Proportion of students entering from low participation neighbour-hoods	49	7	95
Proportion of students entering from lower socio-economic groups	66	2	88

Darwin University looks like the "worst" of these three. It has less well qualified students, relatively few staff for the number of students it has, a high drop out rate (relatively low proportion who complete), fewer of its graduates get graduate level jobs and is about middle of the table as far as getting a good Honours degree is concerned. We know the real university quite well and can account for many of its "failings".

It specialises in taking in what have become known as "non-traditional students": students who have studied access or foundation courses, students who do not appear on the A level score map, students from areas of the country from which Higher Education recruits very poorly.

The staff are extremely supportive and many give a high priority to their teaching. Darwin gives chances to many students that other universities do not and not all make the grade – but at least they had the chance. Should Chris go to Darwin? Well if she has "non traditional" entrance qualifications, and wants to study an applied subject, and if the course at Darwin has those components that she values, then yes she definitely should.

In choosing a university, change is stimulating but it can also be uncomfortable. So you need to ask yourself about Chris's background. Did you or she *expect* her to be going to university? Do you live in an area from which few young people go on to Higher Education? Would Chris be more comfortable mixing in a group of people from the same background or would she rise to the challenge of a different social culture?

A university taking in students from "under-represented groups", like Darwin, actually takes in a large number of students from lower socio-economic groups and from postcode areas that traditionally have sent few students into Higher Education. Thus Darwin is high in the rankings for these characteristics. Teaching in Darwin is going to be sympathetic to the needs of students from these backgrounds.

So Darwin is not "worse" than Pasteur University, it is merely different. If those different characteristics suit Chris then she should think seriously about Darwin as a destination. You need to look at the individual characteristics within a league table, therefore, and select only those that are important to you and Chris.

The question is not "How did all those *other* students get on at Fleming University?" it should be "How will *Chris* get on at Fleming?" If Chris is not like many of those other students then her expectations might be different. Chris should be matching herself to the institution, not only by subject and likely grade, but also by how she would like to be assessed, and the sorts of students currently at the institution. Basically she should go and have a look for herself. Also think carefully about how league tables may be compiled.

Note in our examples that we didn't define "good Honours degrees" or "low participation" or "lower socio-economic groups". Real league tables can be equally vague. In some league tables, spending on library facilities has been taken into account, but consider the university that decided to invest in electronic sources of information, rather than buying expensive hard copy issues of research journals. It saved money and freed up library space. The money was spent on bursaries for students. But the university dropped in the league tables because the "library spend" measure went down.

Similarly, consider the university that leased all its computers. They were repaired when necessary and all replaced every three years. The university saved a fortune, but it had a score of zero computers per student because it didn't actually own any! Again it dropped in the tables. Most of all remember that league tables measure universities, not courses. Some league tables have attempted to compare subjects across universities, but courses are often so different that the comparisons make little sense. The league tables don't tell you this bit.

If you are thinking that Chris should aim to go to the 'best' university she can, and you are basing what is best on the entry requirements, then think again. In 2003/4 the published entry standards at UK universities ranged from 170 to 525 UCAS tariff points, or in A level terms about CD to AAAA, but remember that universities will accept students with lower grades through the "clearing" process. The entry grades do not tell you much about the quality of the teaching; they only tell you that many well-qualified applicants end up at some institutions and courses while many less well-qualified students end up at others. They may also tell you something about how well a university is likely to fill its course and whether it is a selecting, recruiting or sink course.

Some universities ask for high entry grades to make prospective students think they are applying to a high quality course. It's all about brand image. Chris should choose the course she wants to do, irrespective of the asking grades. The entry requirements can tell you nothing about Chris's chances of success.

Some information on the quality of teaching is, however, available on the UK government's Teaching Quality Information website (*www.tqi.ac.uk*). The information comes both from the results of surveys of students during their final year and from official statistics. The surveys are snapshots of the experience of a sample of students.

Remember that their first year was three or four years ago and things may have changed since then. In addition the TQI website will allow you to estimate class size and the job prospects of graduates, and to compare data between groups of courses at specific universities.

It sounds powerful, and is, but remember that personal experience often outweighs official or unofficial statistics, especially when you don't know exactly how those statistics were compiled. The importance of the TQI website is likely to grow as new information is added to it.

The UK's Quality Assurance Agency (*www.qaa.ac.uk*) regularly audits universities to provide "public information on the quality of the opportunities available to students and on the academic standards of awards". You may find information of use on its website, though audits are usually on 6-year cycles and information can quickly become out of date. The audits give an overview of the university as a whole and may not be applicable to the course Chris is interested in.

The QAA's website does, however, have some details on individual courses or groups of courses, but this level of scrutiny is in decline and the information here may be seriously out of date. The websites of both TQI and the QAA are just examples of the sources of evidence you need to examine when Chris is choosing a university.

Finishing the application process

First, Chris should get the balance right. Thus far we seem to have forgotten that Chris has other things to do, apart from keeping up with her academic work. That academic work will probably involve a lot of coursework, depending on the qualification. Chris's teachers will probably be experienced in getting their students into university. Take their advice: Chris should do precisely what she is asked to do by her teachers.

Let's briefly consider how the admissions process works from a university perspective. University courses have a limited number of places to fill. If all students to whom a university course offered a conditional place actually achieved the asking grade, then the course would be heavily over-subscribed. University admissions tutors, therefore, often plan to slightly undershoot the number of places they have available on the basis of their past experience of how many students will achieve their asking grades.

When the A level and other examination results come out in August the course then confirms places for all those who have met the conditions and then they select the requisite number of students from those who just missed the grades. So don't be alarmed if Chris has a near miss in obtaining the grades required for university entry: the university might accept her anyway. Courses that still have vacant places, then enter a process known as "clearing" which matches unplaced students to vacant places. Again the UCAS website should be your first port of call.

If Chris finds it necessary to enter clearing then she needs to be careful. Any place is not necessarily better than no place. If Chris is going to take a gap year then there is no hurry. If Chris wishes to enter university immediately then she has a few weeks to find an appropriate place. She has some decisions to make. She has taken some A levels or perhaps a BTEC qualification, researched and applied for a place at a university and been given a conditional offer. They wanted her if she could fulfil the conditions; she wanted to go there. How much of a disappointment is it going to be to go to a different place or study a different subject? But she does not have to go to university now.

If she only just missed the grades she should consider retaking some courses and trying again next year. If she does decide to go straight to university then she needs to decide what subject she wishes to study and where to study it. In clearing, her location can be specific (i.e. a particular university) or general (for example in the north-west of England). The best thing for her to do is to use the UCAS website to contact the universities that have places and are in the region in which she wishes to study.

She shouldn't go blindly through the application process. She should talk to the staff, visit the campus, and find out as much as she can about the place and the course. Provided she starts the process quickly there will be time, but she will need your help both as a sounding board and, most probably, as a taxi driver.

Research shows us that those students who enter through clearing are the most likely to be in the group that choose to leave early. Interpretations abound, but one obvious conclusion would be that such students had set their hearts on going somewhere else and the university that they actually end up at does not live up to the expectations formed about their first choice.

Further, maybe they didn't do their homework and may not even have been there before they arrived for the first day of study. Chris needs to take as much care about selecting an institution and course during clearing as she did when she initially applied.

And finally ...

Here's an example concerning a friend of ours who passionately wanted to study Law. He didn't make the grade to study it at his chosen university but that university offered him a place on a German course that was firmly in the recruiting class of courses. But he persisted with his intention to study Law and switched universities at the last minute. He did very well and is now studying to be a barrister, but how different things would have been had he been tempted by the course in German.

We've tried to show the critical events in the timeline before Chris enters university. But Chris is an individual and her 'critical points' might not be the same as someone else's. Can you identify the critical points for your 'Chris'?

Chapter 3

Student timeline: at university and beyond

So Chris has got her place to study at university. Congratulations! What happens now? Again we'll take you through the 'standard' steps Chris is likely to take, illustrating the critical events. We'll also consider 'standard' parent steps. Do you remember when she went on that trip that the school organised and she was sent a list of things to take? Changes of this, changes of that, sewing name tags into her underwear and all that sort of thing?

Entering into university is not quite like that. The university won't give that sort of detail and neither will we... it's all about independence. She will receive an acceptance from her chosen course. They will say that she has a place, maybe a welcoming message from the head of the university, the vice-chancellor, saying how lucky she is, and there will be details of possible accommodation. If Chris will be living at the university as opposed to living at home then getting accommodation will obviously be essential. Let's deal with that first.

Accommodation

For first year students who are living away from home, the university will normally take the initiative in allocating accommodation, either in university halls of residence or in university-approved accommodation outside the campus. Applying for accommodation is a simple process and before she goes to the university Chris (and you) will know where she will be living. The university may offer her only one choice, and she will probably have to commit to staying there for the whole academic year.

Although university accommodation is generally fairly basic, it's usually secure and well-maintained. We know this because outside term time many universities run conferences and delegates stay in university halls of residence. So we do have recent experience of living in such places, albeit briefly. A few rooms are en suite, many, but not all, halls provide meals, and most will have some shared facilities for the preparation of food.

Find out exactly what is available – Chris might have a choice if she acts quickly. If possible she should 'case the joint' a couple of weeks before term starts. One of our sons did this and it greatly influenced what was packed. The accommodation staff were very helpful when he asked to see the room he'd be living in. Finding out will help you, at least, in planning what items Chris should take.

Joining instructions

As the first term approaches, Chris will receive joining instructions from the university. These will tell her precisely when and where to go and what she needs to bring. If she is going to be living in university accommodation there will also be details about collecting keys and that sort of thing. The 'what to bring' part is not about personal belongings. It is about evidence of the qualifications she may have gained, a birth certificate, and evidence about how the fees are going to be paid, for example.

Joining instructions will also include who to see about the academic side of university: enrolling on modules, who to get advice from, often an appointment with an individual member of staff. Remember that although Chris will not have been to university before, those who administer these systems have been doing it for years and this process all runs very smoothly indeed. All Chris needs to do is to follow the instructions precisely.

Often the joining instructions will include an invitation for parents or family to attend events on the days during which new students enrol. The purpose of this is two-fold. First, universities realise that many new students will be brought to the campus by their parents (often with a car full of luggage) with, perhaps, younger siblings. Some of the processes involved in registration can be tedious and need not involve parents. Rather than have parents and families hanging around, such special events are organised for them. It is a humane thing to do.

The second purpose is to make parents feel included in the institution. Universities know that Chris may not be your only, or even your youngest, child and the better impression they can make, the more likely you are to encourage other family members to apply to them in the future.

Furthermore, parents/guardians and other family members have an enormous influence over young students and a parent who has been included in activities is more likely to offer support than one who has not. So there may be an induction for family members and if there is, then attend it. It will be a further opportunity to ask questions and will give you a chance to learn some of the geography and personalities of the institution, which Chris may be discussing in the months and years to come.

If no formal induction for parents is offered then seize the initiative and have a wander around to get a 'feel' for the place. Visit the library (often nowadays referred to as the learning resource centre or similar), the refectories, the coffee bars, the sports facilities, or whatever you fancy. In this way you'll be in a better position to understand Chris when she shares with you tales of her on-campus exploits! If Chris is going to a university away from home then at the very least you will become familiar with the town and the route to it.

What to take

If Chris is going to live away from home then you and she will need to think carefully about what she takes. Advise her not to take too much 'stuff'. Most student accommodation is cramped compared with what she might have been used to at home. She will need to store all that she takes in her room and typically a room will have a small wardrobe, a desk and a bed.

You will be told what the accommodation provides but normally the bare cooking utensils will already be there. Bed linen is normally provided as is some crockery and cutlery. If she is a whiz with a wok then she needs to take one of her own. She should not take anything she does not need or cannot afford to lose, because most students have a very open interpretation of sharing when it comes to kitchen items.

Chris can expect to have easy access to laundry facilities so it is not necessary to take enough clean clothes for 12 weeks, but some elementary training in the use of a washing machine, a tumble dryer and (depending on the clothes) an iron will be necessary. Remember that she will be going in September/October and may not be back until December: as the weather changes she will need a range of clothes. Also do not forget *where* she is going. The weather in Aberdeen is not the same as that in Exeter.

The days of very formal events at university are gone for most students so clothes should be comfortable rather than stylish but she should be prepared for some smart casual occasions. Remember, however, that most universities are not all in one building and residences and lodgings may well be several miles from the teaching facilities – a route may need to be planned.

She will certainly be using computers no matter what subject she studies. So one that is personal to her will be a help, but isn't essential. Computers are increasingly used by students to access information on the internet, to prepare assignments, to communicate with friends and academic staff, etc.

The university will provide computing facilities but there will never be enough. The university may have a scheme to sell or lease computers to students. These will normally be cheaper than the high street prices so if she does not have one already, and she wants one, then it may be best to leave it until she gets to university. Also, for certain degree courses there may be a requirement to run particular software, so the specification of the computer may be important too.

Remember that students can get student versions of many common software packages, e.g. Microsoft Office, from most computer shops. Often universities themselves offer standard packages to students at 'knock-down' prices. Check all these things out in advance!

The best sort of computer to have is a laptop. She can take this wherever she needs to work and, increasingly, universities are developing WiFi areas so that access to the internet and e-mail is available without having to plug the machine into a socket. Much university accommodation is now WiFi enabled too.

On average students take about £4500-worth of goods with them to university. This may seem a lot but when you include the computer, a printer, a mobile phone, MP3 player, books and clothes, it soon adds up. Some of this may be covered on your own home insurance but you need to check because policies vary.

You can take out student cover for items the typical student would possess and for the risks that the typical student would face. The National Union of Students (*www.nusonline.co.uk*) has information on its website which directs you to the insurance company it founded – other insurance companies are available! If Chris is in university-owned accommodation, check the small print – insurance is sometimes included.

Leave quickly!

If Chris is studying away from home then you should leave the university immediately after you have completed your business. Do not look back. Chris will be busy – investigating her new surroundings, making new friends, unpacking, and finding the nearest supermarket or pub. Make sure you know how to contact her: postal address, phone, mobile and e-mail. If Chris has a pay-as-you-go phone then make sure it is topped up.

One of us still tops up his son's pay-as-you-go phone even though he left university years ago. It is a way of ensuring ongoing contact. Our experience has been that daughters are much more likely to maintain regular contact (and we mean daily!) with home than are sons. The only thing to remember is that when she needs help then you will be the first person on the list.

No one tells you what the void created by Chris's leaving is going to be like. There is the excitement of being involved in getting her a place at university, deciding what to take, packing up the suitcases and the car, driving to the campus, finding where everything is. And then she is gone; you are driving back, sometimes alone, sometimes through areas you have never been through before, often as the sun is going down.

She will be fine; she is still caught up in the excitement of it all. You might be the one with the problem. You need to prepare for this moment and the weeks and months and years to come as you adjust to these new circumstances.

Empty nest syndrome

We know that this book is about getting Chris through university but you will be of no help to her if you are not comfortable with her being away and have trouble adjusting *your* life to *her* new-found freedom. The loss of a child to university, even though it may be temporary, can be an emotional experience for many parents, especially mothers. Some are more susceptible than others. It is worth considering if you recognise any of the following.

• Do you view change as a stressful, rather than a challenging or refreshing experience? Have you found, for instance, moving house emotionally difficult?

• Were events such as weaning, or Chris's first day at school difficult experiences for you?

• Do you think of yourself as Chris's Mum or Dad, or as a wife or a husband, rather than thinking of yourself as an individual?

• Do you have other roles as well as that of a parent (e.g. do you work, care for other family members, etc.)?

• Do you think that Chris is not really old enough to leave home?

If you are answering 'yes' to most of these, then you need to plan for Chris's leaving home. It is likely to have a worse effect on you than on her. The most stressful things are those where you would like both of two opposing things to happen.

In this case you might want Chris to go to university. It is a step towards a worthwhile career and will allow her to make the best of her talents. On the other hand you might also want her not to go to university and to stay at home. She is becoming good company, she helps around the home, and if she got a job she could help make ends meet. Both outcomes are good for you in different ways, but you can have only one.

Aside from the stress of not getting what you want, 'empty-nesting' is a sort of grieving process and all those things that apply to the loss of a loved one also apply to empty nest syndrome. So it is OK to feel upset but you need to talk it through with your partner, close friends, or relatives: people you trust or who have been through it themselves.

You might need deliberately to establish a new sort of relationship with Chris and perhaps other adult children, one which is less possessive and more like the sorts of close friendships you might have developed with other family members. You might also need to re-establish the closeness of the relationship with your partner that was there before Chris entered your lives, and work to occupy those spaces in your routine that were taken up with your role as a parent.

Above all, if you are prone to empty nest syndrome then you will need to cope with those around you who will keep telling you how lucky you are now that you are free of parental responsibilities.

There are a number of actions you can take to counter the worst effects of empty nest syndrome. First, accept it for what it normally is – a short-term reaction to a sudden change in circumstances. Do not make big changes in your life, like moving house, until you have adapted to these changes. Second, you know that this is going to happen so plan for it. You want to help Chris get her place and go to university but you also need to prepare yourself for her not being there.

Even if she is going to be living at home, you will be seeing a lot less of her in future and her priorities will change over time. She may for instance choose to live away from home even though she could stay. This is relatively common and shows that Chris is gaining in independence, but how is that going to affect you?

What can you do about it? People obviously vary and we cannot tell you precisely what will suit you and your circumstances. The following is a short list of actions that others have taken in response to empty-nesting.

- Most of us have an unwritten list of things we always wanted to do. Now's the time to write it out! You may not have had time for hobbies and pastimes in recent years. Now might be your chance.
- Remember that the longest journey starts with a single step, so start by setting yourself small achievable goals.
- Renew contacts with friends, neighbours and relations.
- Join a club or group (just as Chris is probably doing to help her settle), or get a part-time job if you are not working already.
- Start volunteering. There is a whole host of organisations looking for volunteers. This will extend your social contacts and renew your perspectives on life.
- Finally, if you are still upset after Chris has been away for several months, or if you feel overwhelmed then seek professional guidance – your GP is a first port of call.

Settling in

DOMESTIC ARRANGEMENTS

Well that's enough about you! Chris is the focus of our attention and we are concerned about you because your distress and apparent disapproval might affect the way in which Chris adapts to life at university. What will happen when you have driven off, leaving Chris behind?

Many universities operate a peer guiding system in which experienced students 'buddy up' with new students. This system works really well and if Chris is offered a peer guide then she should accept the opportunity. Peer guiding is just one of the phrases used to describe this buddy system which may operate formally or informally in universities.

It might also be known as peer mentoring, college aunts or uncles or some other family member, or just simply as buddying. Whatever it is called encourage Chris to participate, first now as a new student and also later when a new crop of students need support. There is nothing like help from someone who has just done what you are about to do, to show you how easy things can be and what you need to worry about and what is trivial. Here are a few of the things new students have said about their guides.

"Within minutes of my arrival my Peer Guide came to see me. I had a few initial questions and she was able to help. What she didn't know she went and found out and got back to me within an hour ... She took us all on a tour of the local nightlife ... Throughout Freshers' week she popped up every day to see if I was OK and answer any questions. Then she was a constant source of support for the rest of the semester, always there to answer questions. She even walked us all the way home at 3 a.m. when we didn't know our way back ... She was so friendly and approachable, not once did I feel silly asking her questions ... She even sent me a message on Christmas day wishing me a happy Christmas."

CASE STUDY – TRACY
A sample of Tracy's first afternoon after having

been left in her room at university by her parents.

3:30 p.m. Well, they have gone and I am all alone in my room. I'm absolutely miserable and close to tears. What on earth am I doing in this small room in this strange place when I could be at home? I wish my boyfriend was here. He'd cheer me up.

3:40 p.m. There is a knock on the door. I straighten my hair and dab away the tears. I open my door for the first time. "Hello! We're your peer guides!" Two girls have come to see if I am OK and within a few minutes we are chatting away. They suggest we go downstairs to the cafe and off we go.

5:00 p.m. Back alone in my room again. I've agreed to meet my guides again later on to see what is going on in the town.

7.25 p.m. I'm lost. Someone pointed me in this direction but I'm sure it can't be right. I should have brought the map. Everybody else is going the other way! My Peer Guides told me to meet them at 7.30 p.m. – at this rate I'll never find them!

8.20 p.m. I return to my room for a defeated cup of tea. I go along to the communal kitchen and put the kettle on. I flop down on the kitchen sofa and explain my very tragic evening to my floor mates. "We're off out" they say, "Would you like to tag along?" Well, in my present mood anything is better than staying in.

3.15 a.m. Back in my room again. What an evening! The other girls on my floor are quite good fun. I think I will like living here. They had attended some sort of early induction programme a few weeks ago so knew each other from before. We ended up at a club called Johnny's and danced till the early hours. I laughed my head off – it must have been the *relief of not being alone. And I even found my Peer Guides as well!*

What can you learn about settling in from Tracy's story? The first thing is that Chris should join in. If there are activities organised by the university before the formal start of term then you should encourage Chris to go. If there is an opportunity to have a peer guide then she should take it. If there is a communal kitchen then she should make extensive use of it. If there is a group going out then she should go with them. University is a social experience as well as an academic one. And to get the best out of it Chris needs to join in.

The second thing is that Chris might well be miserable in the first few days and weeks of being away. For all but a few students, this will pass.

The third thing is that relationships made before university often don't last at university. Be prepared for the boyfriend or girlfriend or indeed Chris to be 'dumped'. Your emotional support here could be critical. Harsh, but it is unlikely that a youthful relationship will outweigh the desire to complete a university course or to keep company with those embarked on a similar path.

ACADEMIC ARRANGEMENTS

The initial experience of students at university is probably of being overwhelmed by new information. Academic staff will write a lot of information and instructions down and give it to new students in the first week. They may well believe that is the job done.

The information has been given – students should know it. Chris will need to cope with this attitude. She may be expected to know and act on a lot of different bits of paper she has been given. It is surprising how many students are missing in classes at the beginning of the first term. It is not that they have not been given the right information, it is that they have not found, read or understood it. You would think that academic staff would learn, but sometimes we do not. After their induction, one of us contacted the whole group of Biology students by e-mail to remind them of the next week's lecture. Here is one e-mail we got in reply.

"Thanks for the e-mail. I did attend the induction lecture but as our timetable overlapped with many other classes I wasn't sure whether to attend or not so I went to the lecture room and asked the lady there but she didn't know if the biology students were supposed to be there, but I took a handbook just in case. Will be there next Fri. and thanks again."

She had gone to the right place but even the staff did not know if she was supposed to be there. The first week can be chaotic for individual students! It may not seem like that to staff because most students get it right; the staff have not met this group of students before and do not know what to expect. We do not have registers like schools do; in general we do not count students in and out of class.

Because of the flexible arrangements involved in joining a university, it will be unlikely that the teaching staff will have a definitive list of students doing the course. So when Chris tells you about uncertainty in the first few weeks then just imagine the sorts of panic *we* get into. With an operation the size of a university class, mistakes are inevitable; it is actually no one's fault and quickly gets sorted out. Missing one or two sessions is not critical and provided Chris manages to get on track fairly quickly there will have been no harm done.

She should not, however, miss what we call 'induction'. This may not sound important but this will be a series of events in the first week during which she will get some critical information, including where she has to be and when. She will be told about what to do if she has personal or financial difficulties, how to access university computers, her e-mail address and so forth.

She will be told about aspects of student discipline, such as the consequences of missing classes or plagiarism. Above all, induction is an opportunity for staff to get to know new students and for students to recognise the staff with whom they will be working over the next few years. Induction is critical: it represents an opportunity to find things out without having to search through all the handbooks that she will have been given and also to familiarise herself with people in the bit of the university in which she will be working.

The university lifestyle

LIVING WITH OTHERS

In the first year Chris will not be able to choose with whom she will be living (though that will change in later years). This could be a test of her ability to tolerate others and will certainly represent a very steep learning curve, especially if she is an only child. Our advice is for her to find somewhere quiet to work, to join a group of friends whose company she enjoys, and to form a learning community of people from the same course with whom she can discuss her work.

These things sound more difficult and daunting than they actually are and may all be centred around her accommodation, but not necessarily. Most students find that the bonds formed in those first few weeks of university life will last a long time, and many students thrown together apparently at random by an accommodation officer will be friends for life.

If Chris is living away for the first time, what should you warn her about? The first thing is that petty things will grow. When a small group is living together then the person who uses all the butter without replacing it or who does not do their share of the washing-up can become very unpopular.

She might need reminding that she is joining a small community of equals. Everyone should expect to do everything – but you and Chris should be prepared for this not to be the case. There is unlikely to be a mother/father figure who will clean up or make sure the fridge is well-stocked. The advice to give Chris is "if everyone involved behaved in the same way as you, would everyone be happy?" – a small variation on the maxim – "do as you would be done by".

Chris will mature fast at university, so expect to see some changes in her. Nevertheless, keep your parental radar alert because some students don't handle their new-found freedom too well. Universities are not dens of iniquity when it comes to casual sex, binge drinking and illegal drugs – we'll pass over our personal experiences at this point – but the temptation may be there for young people in a new environment.

If you detect changes that you think might be outside the normal 'maturing' process, it might be worth mentioning to Chris the support services that universities provide for their students (see Chapter 8 *Student support services*).

RELATIONSHIPS AT HOME

Only you can judge how much contact with Chris is appropriate. She may make a lot of contact in the early weeks of her course and this may then decline. We know of students who phone their mums every day and of some who hardly ever phone home at all. It is likely that Chris's lifestyle will change. She will be doing things differently at university from when she was at home.

You cannot control that, nor should you try to. The sorts of difficulties that Chris will have will probably revolve around the strangeness of her new environment and new ways of working at university for which she may be ill-prepared, but these will pass.

She may also have problems maintaining what are essentially two lives. She is living for about half the year at university with its associated workload, freedom and social contacts, and the other half at home with its support and emotional commitments. She may need your support and approval so that one life does not intrude too much on the other.

Chris may of course be living at home; an increasing number of students choose to live in the parental home while studying. Their experience of university will obviously be different from 'boarding' students. As she gets more deeply involved with the university side of her life, you will have to be more flexible about your demands on her time and attention.

VISITING HOME

Students living away from home will visit home with varying frequency. Often the weekend jobs they had while at school will be maintained and this will mean that they go home every weekend. Some will get part-time jobs in the university town and will not be free to go home. Students go home for a variety of other reasons: to get their washing done; to retreat to a familiar environment; to see boy/girl friends; to help in the family business. You should try to maintain home as a safe place to which Chris can retreat.

Part-time work

Students never have enough money and Chris is unlikely to be any different. There is a social life to maintain, books and other equipment to buy, commuting to and from the campus, and long holidays to plan. Some students still sponge off their parents but more frequently they will get part-time jobs to increase their income.

What are you going to advise Chris when she asks about whether to apply for or accept a job? In general, working part-time is a good thing provided that the time is limited and that it does not impinge on her academic work. We find that students who work part-time are able to develop many of the work-based skills which we find difficult to engender within an academic curriculum (see Chapter 11 *What next?*).

Work will impress the need for discipline, especially time keeping, and develop a client-centred approach. Thus we find that work is beneficial: but only up to a point. Students who spend too much time in part-time work will neglect their studies and their performance will suffer. So encourage Chris to seek work but to be sensible about the amount of time she commits to it and the priority she gives it, especially during term time. This can be difficult as many employers, such as supermarkets for example, think that students are very flexible and they can make excessive and inappropriate demands on a student's time – talk things through with Chris to work out what might be best for her.

The first thing Chris should do is to find out if the university itself has a job shop. Getting work through a university-sponsored organisation will ensure that she is not committed to too many hours or hours that are unsocial.

Remember that the university curriculum is designed to occupy a student for about 40 hours a week. That will tend to be loaded towards the end of the terms or semesters when assessment becomes more intense, but this figure still makes a good basis on which to plan. Weekend work and evening work are the best choices. Working during the normal working day might impinge on her ability to attend academic sessions and although few courses insist that all sessions are attended (though many insist that *some* are attended), no student should make commitments that result in repeated non-attendance.

Another aspect to consider is the stage that Chris is at in her course. In her final year she will be committed to extensive reading, especially in support of a research project or dissertation. This is critical study and if Chris finds it necessary to work to support herself then it is best to build up reserves early in the course so that the outside work can be curtailed later in the course.

So our advice on outside work is for you to encourage it, especially in the early years but only to a limited extent. With a social life, academic life and a work life this will be the most complicated time of Chris's life so far and she will need to balance the demands on her time so that her long term future is not sacrificed to her short term needs.

Progression

Chris will progress from year to year on the basis of her assessment results (see Chapter 6 *Assessment*), though she may have some hiccups along the way. At best this will be not doing as well as she expected; at worst, she may fail and have to repeat a year or leave entirely. None of these less than perfect outcomes is a tragedy. Remember we are now living in an era of life-long learning.

As a mature student (over 19) many new opportunities open up and some of the restrictions on entry to university are removed. If Chris does fail or drop out of university then this will be taken into account when she is assessed for funding for a new course, so she may not be able to get a loan for the total time for her second time around.

Mixes of part-time and full-time study might open up for her so that she can study full-time for the more taxing part of the course and part-time for the introductory parts. The complications of funding aside, mature students often do better than when they were younger because they tend to be more focused and better motivated than their younger selves. We cannot stress enough that doors will not close on her. For more information see Chapter 10 *Avoiding and recovering from a poor start*.

Work placement – the sandwich option

Many courses, and not just vocational (work-related) courses, offer students the opportunity to undertake a period of work-based learning, often called a placement. These may be relatively short, being just a week or two, or may be for three months or for a whole year.

In this last case, the course is often referred to as a sandwich degree as it sandwiches the period of work experience between two periods at university. In a three-year course the placement would normally be between years two and three. Some universities call these placements 'industrial placements', but 'industry' is interpreted loosely to include charitable organisations, educational establishments, field centres, government agencies, and even other universities. Some of these schemes also allow for work or study abroad.

Thus, during year two, many students are offered the option of undertaking a placement year at the end of the year, delaying entry to their final year until placement is completed. In some courses, placements may be compulsory because of the nature of the course, while in many others a year's placement is offered as an option.

Our advice... if Chris is doing a course where placement is an option then encourage her to do it. Yes, we know this means it will take her another year to complete her degree and that her university may well charge half-fees for that year, but the experience obtained is invaluable – see CASE STUDY – KEVIN in Chapter 11 *What next?*

Evidence suggests that students who take a placement between years two and three do better in their final year than those who choose not to. Direct comparisons like this are always difficult as it might be argued that the brighter students will tend to be the ones who take a placement. But, even better than just a straight improvement in marks, is the change seen in aspects such as time-management, professional attitude towards work, enthusiasm, motivation, etc. It is very obvious to us which students in final year classes have completed a placement and which have not.

We repeat the advice. If there is the opportunity to take a placement then encourage Chris to give it very serious thought. Talk through the issues with Chris. Remember that she may be paid for her placement year (currently the rates are about £10,000 to £15,000) and she might be able to use some of this money to pay back some of her student loan – though some placements are unpaid and the student chooses to do them for the experience rather than the cash.

Another distinct advantage might be that it acts as a negative-positive experience in that the post may not be to Chris's liking and she may then decide it is *not* a career path she wishes to pursue on graduation. We have known a number of students in this category... it has helped students make much more positive and informed decisions after graduation.

Similarly, most universities operate a variety of exchange schemes with other universities, usually abroad. These schemes may be run by the universities concerned, or may be part of various national, EU and international programmes. They do not typically extend a student's period of study because the study away from the university 'counts' as part of the student's course. But they do offer the opportunity to study in a different environment, broadening experience and providing good CV fodder. Financial support may also be available. If Chris is interested in doing part of her course at another university, she should find out about this early.

Dropping out

Persistence is a quality which is highly valued by employers and dropping out is often equated with giving up. We know from wide experience that dropping out is more often associated with having made bad choices either about the course or the institution and we also know that many students who drop out actually drop back in fairly rapidly and complete a degree either in another subject or at another university.

Most students who drop out do so within the first few months of being at university. You will know if Chris is going to survive the university experience within a very few weeks of her joining the course. If she starts to miss classes, spends too much time at home and does not seem to be focused on academic work, then she will be drifting towards early leaving.

Students of Chris's age do not leave suddenly; they slowly disengage from study as they become disillusioned with their lot. The work appears to become too difficult, she is not liked by fellow students, the staff ignore her needs, the social activities are too much trouble or at the wrong time, she does not know where to go. These are all signs that she has not actually joined in and is one reason why we emphasise 'joining in' so much.

The place may actually be foreign to her; her classmates may all be living at home and she is living away so she never sees anyone; they may all have A level Chemistry and she never even had the opportunity to take it so she feels she cannot cope; she thought the course carried professional recognition and she has just discovered that it does not, so her employment prospects are not as good as she had been led to believe.

There are thousands of good reasons why Chris should leave but most of them were there before she enrolled. However, Chris may have very good reasons not to continue on the course and non-continuance does not necessarily equal failure.

If Chris is determined to drop out then encourage her to drop out positively. That is, not so much to drop out as to choose to do something else. She should be making positive and optimistic choices. She can choose to get a job to save up and fund herself on a more suitable course. She can choose to enhance her entrance qualifications so she can get into the course she wanted to do in the first place. There are all sorts of choices she can make and the only one she should not make is the choice to do nothing. Lend a supportive and non-judgemental ear.

Graduation and careers

Once over the first few weeks most students will progress through the course without major mishap. A few drop out later and a few will fail academically, but these tend to be a very small minority. It is most likely that Chris will progress to her final examinations and graduate.

Strangely, universities celebrate students leaving much more than they celebrate their arrival. When Chris finishes at university and 'graduates' you will be able to go along to a ceremonial event – graduation – to mark the occasion. Chris will be awarded the degree whether she goes to the ceremony or not, but it's usually a good event for proud parents/guardians to go to.

For now, you might like to know how the university will ultimately judge Chris. As we've already said, there are various types of degree. The most common 'first' degree, i.e. the one students study for first, as opposed to one they might study for later in their careers, is the Honours degree. Currently UK universities don't issue students with an overall precise mark, such as a percentage, when an Honours degree is awarded, although there is a move to do this. Instead they group marks together in bands or *classifications*.

Historically there were three pass classifications: students gaining the best marks were awarded a First Class Honours Degree (or simply a First, 1st or I); those slightly below, a Second Class Honours Degree (or a Second, 2nd or II); and those lower still, a Third Class Honours Degree (or a Third, 3rd or III). However, so many students were graduating with Second Class awards that this classification was split into two: an Upper Second (2_i, 2_I, or II_I) and a Lower Second (2_{ii}, 2_{II}, or II_{II}).

Roughly, but only roughly because individual universities have much discretion at the boundaries and because some universities use grade points instead of percentages, the relationship between percentages and classifications goes something like this:

First Class	70 – 100 %;
Upper Second Class	60 – 69 %;
Lower Second Class	50 – 59 %;
Third Class	40 – 49 %;
Fail	0 – 39 %.

These days universities tend to issue students with transcripts of their marks so they could, in theory, calculate their overall final percentage. But university regulations are often labyrinthine, combining marks from various years of study and applying weightings to different parts of the programme, so the calculation often isn't so straightforward.

All the above applies only to Honours degrees, the most common type. Other types of degree, for example, in Medicine, are not classified at all: students either pass or fail. For degrees carrying accreditation by professional bodies, the pass mark may be higher. For others, the professional body may insist that the first degree is at Masters level: typically a four-year course. It's complex. Make sure you and Chris know what type of degree she's studying for.

So imagine Chris has made it through university. You might be relieved and think that the job is done. In reality only the first phase of Chris's on-going education is complete. We'll leave the details of careers and their planning to Chapter 11 *What next?*

For now we'll say that universities devote considerable time and effort into preparing students for the great world of employment, and offer the following as food for thought. One of our sons did a degree in Computer Science, and a very fine computer scientist he is. But it was being the secretary of the University Dead Parrot Society which taught him how to prepare minutes, how to organise meetings and how to persuade people not to say "no". We're sure the 'joining in' did him the world of good – especially in getting his foot on the career ladder.

And finally …

This is the end of our timeline. It didn't say much about Chris's academic experiences at university – that's for the next chapters. But hopefully you're in a better position to realise where the crunch points – our critical events – lie and to predict them and to plan for them.

Chapter 4

What it's like at university

Psychologists tell us that the most stressful times in life are divorce and moving house. For Chris, going to university can be a bit like divorcing her parents and may involve moving house too. She is bound to be at least a little stressed, even if this is contained within clouds of euphoria and perhaps freedom. To get a feel for her situation, imagine you are on your own and you have moved house to a big city – think of one – that you do not know at all.

You moved house on Sunday and start a new job on Monday. You know a little about the job, but not much. You want to create a good impression. Get the picture? Chris will need someone to talk to when she gets there, someone she can rely on to give her good advice. You can best support Chris in this transition by knowing something about life at university. Universities are worlds apart from any other education or training system – including, and perhaps especially, schools. Here's why …

The university village

University campuses come in lots of forms. There are the large city-centre campuses concentrated mostly on one site like the Universities of Leeds and Glasgow. There are those city universities that are distributed through the geography of the whole town like the Universities of Sunderland, Cambridge and Queen's Belfast. There are green field universities set in their own grounds like the Universities of Lancaster and Sussex.

There are the specialist colleges in rural settings like Harper Adams University College and Dartington

College of Arts. Some universities are in between and some are a combination of these artificial categories. No matter what type of campus, however, universities tend to be village-like in that they contain just about all the elements Chris could require for a complete academic and social life. Post Offices and banks on campus are not unusual, and bars, sports centres and student accommodation are the norm. Also present, though perhaps not so obvious are the non-course services the university provides for its students. These can range from help with honing maths and English skills to personal and financial advice.

Chris should be prepared for the physical scale of a university to be much bigger than the school or college she might be used to. It's also busy – Chris shouldn't be daunted by this. But words are cheap and in reality it is likely that she will, to some extent, feel a little lost in it all.

From our personal experiences of being university students ourselves and in guiding students new to university, this feeling of being lost is perfectly normal and will subside once new friendships are developed and Chris gets to know her 'bit' of the university. We don't know of any student who hasn't felt anxious in the first week at university and reassurance from parents at this time can be extremely important.

Staff at universities are always doing research on various things, sometimes including their own students. Surveys of incoming students have shown that they are generally very anxious about their accommodation and who they will have to live with. They worry about cooking, about shopping, about laundry, about time, and about money. In fact, they are worried about practically everything. But don't panic! Just a few weeks later similar surveys asking the same questions of the same students show that, for most, all these anxieties have gone.

Chris will need reassurance but since you may not have been through what she is experiencing, you will need to marshal some information so that you can offer advice from a position of strength.

The vast array of university facilities combined with the independence given to students by universities (see next section) and perhaps by their parents, means that there are lots of opportunities for distraction and no one to call a halt!

Universities typically have many student-run societies. Some are subject specific, and it might be worthwhile Chris joining these because, for example, they may run useful seminars that are open only to members, or offer discounts on textbooks, but it's best to check what's on offer first. Often there will be a wide range of societies catering for diverse interests and based on, for example, religion, politics, sport and careers. Don't be surprised if Chris joins some strange ones – the Dead Parrot Society or the Tellytubbies Club.

A colleague of ours spent many a happy weekend running around a ruined Welsh castle playing real-life dungeons and dragons. Each to his own! The point about student societies is that they are opportunities to form social networks, to join in and to contribute to the variety of campus life. Most have a membership fee so good advice to Chris would be for her to find out as much as she can before parting with her cash; a few societies seem to exist only for the purpose of drinking! Chris's time at university is a chance to explore new ideas and activities outside of academic life.

These opportunities, often at a discounted rate, might never present themselves again: one of us took up parachuting and SCUBA diving at university. Having an interest outside of academic studies often makes potential employers see applicants as more 'rounded' individuals. Indeed when employers are faced with a number of applicants with much the same by way of qualifications, then it can only be these little extras that will make the difference and secure Chris an interview.

Independence, independence, independence

ACADEMIC INDEPENDENCE

Of course, a student's experience at university will depend on the institution and course chosen, but the one inescapable fact is that that experience will be different from any other form of education or training that Chris has experienced. The key difference lies in the independence of the student; we'll return to this theme often. University lecturers and other staff are, of course, there to help, but usually see themselves not as teachers, but rather as "facilitators" in a learning process.

This might come as a shock to you and even more so to Chris. Don't let it. Think about it instead. In a successful professional career individuals are expected to take responsibility for their own actions, potentially including powerful decision-making. So doesn't it make sense to encourage university students to be capable of learning on their own? Or at least for them not to rely on being spoon-fed?

However, producing the professionals of tomorrow, or "future captains of industry", if you like, doesn't happen overnight, so complete independence isn't expected at first. University staff know that new students are not necessarily independent learners when they arrive.

School assessment systems tend to be teacher-dependent and risk averse: teachers can leave little to chance when their own performance is measured by the examination performance of their pupils. Thus at school, assessments tend to be frequent, often cover only a limited amount of material at a time, and are set in the context of a highly specialised and well-defined curriculum.

When Chris graduates and joins the real world she will have to be an autonomous individual, able to make her own decisions, defend them and stand by their consequences. This may happen all by itself, but at university we organise what we do so that students will have to bear more and more responsibility for what they do as time goes on. We start this evolutionary process from the beginning but, as a result, many students and parents are alarmed by the apparent lack of guidance given to individual students.

However, we do watch our students carefully and help is to hand when it is asked for. But students are not guided every step of the way. Always remember that at university the onus will be firmly on Chris to manage her own learning, that is to take responsibility for what to learn and when to learn it. For example, it is unlikely that there will be frequent tests at university in order to check that students are on top of their subject. They're left to get on with the learning largely by themselves.

We will provide the opportunities for Chris to learn and develop but we cannot learn for her, just as we will not be at her side to guide her when she gets her first job.

While many schools will be judged on the quality and quantity of the examination grades gained by their students, universities are often judged by the employability of their graduates. Often this means the extent to which they can hit the ground running or can adapt rapidly to new ideas.

Being overprotective of students and coaching them to the highest possible qualifications is not in our own interests if, when they graduate, they cannot cut the mustard in the real world. So we deliberately promote independence by rapidly kicking away the educational crutches – Chris will have to stand on her own.

You might find this a little harsh, but it will be the reality. You can best support Chris by realising that her growing independence is in her own interests, but acknowledging that it can cause stress too.

SOCIAL INDEPENDENCE

For many students, part of becoming independent involves independence from family. That means being independent of you. This is especially true, if Chris is 'going away' to university and living in rented accommodation. You may think that she is already too independent for her own good. But there will be times when she will still need your support, and need someone to listen to her problems and sympathise, rather than criticise.

When Chris goes to university, she will not be the only one whose social circumstances will change. You will have an empty room. This can be quite a wrench: make sure both you and Chris are prepared for it. A little homesickness on Chris's part is almost inevitable and you might not feel too great either.

FINANCIAL INDEPENDENCE

It is worthwhile also making sure that Chris is comfortable with taking control of her own finances, that she knows where her money is, how to get it, and how much she is spending. This is something to be practised before going to university. Preparing a budget and trying to stick to it might help.

If she is not already doing so, you could encourage Chris to take control of her own income and spending, encouraging her to have a small surplus each week or month. It might also help to have personal banking sorted out before she goes to university, but make sure she does not miss the inducements banks offer to students to gain their custom. Rare these days, but we know of a few students who have had to open a bank account in order to deal with a cheque!

Chris's chosen university won't be unsympathetic if she gets into financial or personal difficulties. But she will need to inform the university earlier rather than later if the university is to be able to help. Universities have mechanisms in place to support students who find it difficult to study because of non-academic pressures, from granting short extensions to assessment deadlines to offering advice on a range of topics from finance – small grants or loans may be available to tide students over – and accommodation, to personal issues.

If in doubt, Chris shouldn't be afraid to ask; universities are used to, and prepared for, helping students in this way. Of course Chris might be reluctant to discuss financial or personal problems with you, but at least you can point her in the right direction if she does, or if your parent-sense tells you something is wrong. For more information see Chapter 8 *Student support services.*

Maturity

Parents are used to receiving feedback about how well (or badly) their offspring is doing. Regular school reports arrived in the past (addressed to "The Parents or Guardians of Chris" – note the recipients, not Chris but *YOU*) and no doubt you received invitations at least once a year and often more frequently to talk through Chris's performance with the form teacher or subject specialists.

These meetings could be very beneficial and you probably came away from them with a sense of elation ("Chris is predicted to get two As and a C at A2 level"; Wow!). On the other hand, if Chris was performing less well the message might be starker but nevertheless important … "try to persuade Chris to do more reading of the set text book" or "she needs to take more care with her pronunciation ... can you give her some practice?"

At university, the situation is radically different; suddenly, as a parent, you are out of the loop and the university authorities talk to and negotiate with your offspring and not you. Suddenly, no matter how much you are supporting Chris (financially, spiritually, or whatever), the line of communication has changed and you have been totally left out. Not only that, if you try to make discreet enquiries about how well Chris is performing from the module coordinator or course director you will receive a polite but rather firm put-down.

And why should this be so? Nearly all university undergraduates are over 18 years old and universities therefore treat them as independent adults. No matter how much, in your eyes, Chris is still a babe in arms, to a university she is an adult and responsible for all her own actions, no matter what the consequences.

For the university, talking to you about Chris would be a breach of confidentiality. Thus your enquiries about examination and coursework marks, attendance or anything else to do with 'how well' Chris is doing will be met by a well-placed cold shoulder. (And this will extend to other aspects of Chris's life ... health, disciplinary matters, etc.)

There is no doubt that 'pushy' parents can be a pain in the neck for both academics and students. Sometimes, this can lead to out-and-out hostility erupting between parents and offspring – let us give you one example that occurred recently in our experience.

CASE STUDY – LISA
Lisa came from a rather close-knit family in a rural community and she had two elder brothers. The parents wanted all to do well at university

and, indeed, the two brothers progressed through the system with little trouble, both coming out with good degrees, one in Engineering and one in Business Studies. Lisa wasn't so good and did less well in her A levels than her two brothers and found herself on a Foundation degree (a two year non-Honours degree with, in Lisa's case, the possibility on successful completion to progress to a one year Honours degree 'top-up').

Lisa loved her subject and worked hard but certain aspects, particularly the more mathematical elements, were a real struggle for her. As a consequence, she failed a module in Statistics, Computing and Data Handling and was offered the opportunity to re-take the examination in the summer re-sit period in August. Her parents were absolutely furious. They accused Lisa of wasting her time, not working hard enough and living a full social life at the expense of her academic work.

Life got difficult for Lisa, but worse was to follow. She re-took the examination and ... failed it for the second time. However, the Board of Examiners examined her overall performance and, as there was meritorious work in her other modules, allowed her to proceed to her second year but asked her to take an examination in the module for the third (and last possible) time in the following January.

What should she do? She knew that if she told her parents that she had failed the module again she would probably be removed from university – after all, her parents were paying the fees. Or should she lie and tell them that she had passed the module ... risking the possibility that if she failed the module for the third time she would be asked to leave the course.

Having talked things over with her eldest brother she decided to lie to her parents and take the risk. They were all sweetness and light but for six months she lived a very stressful existence. A weaker character might have given way under the pressure but Lisa was made of stern stuff. Luckily for her she passed and, having overcome that hurdle has now transferred to the Honours course.

However, things could have been different if Lisa had told her parents the truth. The responsibility lies clearly with the students to release information to parents and it is not a university's responsibility.

Interestingly, in Lisa's case, one of her elder brothers also had a re-sit examination in his second year. The parents shrugged their shoulders and thought he'd had an 'off-day'. There were no accusations at all about a debauched lifestyle ... which is another important message ... treat all your children the same.

Universities expect Chris, as a mature person, to be able to get the balance right between study and play. But they don't often state this explicitly. You can! You can support Chris by finding out from her how she's getting on with her studies. Vague responses, a lack of communication, or a lot of time spent at home or in student accommodation may mean the time has come for a more focused, supportive discussion.

Discuss!

Sounds like an exam question, doesn't it? What do you do if you have a problem you cannot solve? You probably seek advice, ask, or discuss it with someone; preferably someone who you think has a greater knowledge or understanding than you. We are hopeless at fixing our run-down cars: we invariably seek the advice of a mechanic. Likewise, if something isn't clear at university Chris should ask and discuss.

This might occur more often than you think. In other forms of education learners are generally issued with all the things they require to learn successfully. But at university we do not do that. As part of the process towards becoming an independent learner, students are required to search out quite a lot of material for themselves. University staff will usually give pointers, but the rest is up to the student. If Chris has a problem at university that she cannot solve by herself, or she has an answer but is not sure that it is correct, she should ask someone. We're not just talking about academic problems here: personal, social and financial problems are included too.

Being a mature and independent learner means Chris should be able to recognise when she has explored as far as she can on her own: at that point she needs help. Seeking help is something we all do in our professional lives. One characteristic that employers say they value in employees is the ability to recognise when a problem has been taken as far as it can and the accompanying nous to seek help and guidance.

So she shouldn't be afraid to ask for help and to discuss problems! Asking questions at university is not seen as a confession of ignorance. It is seen as a willingness to learn. What's more, most university staff like students who ask questions because this shows maturity, that they are thinking about things and have an unwillingness to push a problem around in the dark, or indeed to give up. It shows an ability to formulate questions which is a prerequisite for research and it's likely that at some stage in her course Chris will have an opportunity to express these talents.

It is always beneficial for students to explain what they've tried to do on their own – to demonstrate that they can attack a problem – before admitting – another characteristic of maturity – that they've hit a brick wall. Whatever the problem is, students should be encouraged to discuss it. Sometimes, of course, the research just cannot be done – perhaps when Chris has not been issued with the hand-in date for some assessed work, or the feedback she has received is not enough to help her really understand what she did well and where she went wrong – but she should ask anyway. University staff exist for her benefit. She should use them. She should ask and discuss!

It's probably worth broaching the subject of seeking help and advice with Chris early in her studies. Students often have an element of insecurity about their learning at university because the certainties, facts if you like, that were learned at school have been replaced with a more investigative, open-ended approach where there may be no right answers, or even answers at all. This is normal. But make sure that Chris is confident in seeking solutions. She should ask and discuss!

The range of subjects

Up until the age of sixteen or so, the range of subjects studied at school is deliberately broad, for example the GCSE system in the UK. Beyond that, at A level or Scottish Highers, there is a free choice of subjects and that too can be broad compared with what a student will study at university. Once a university course has been selected there may still be some choice available but it would rarely be as broad as that previously experienced.

For example, if Chris is studying a course in French, she may previously have studied French, English and History, and possibly some science or technology related subjects as well. She should not be surprised therefore that the subject(s) she studies at university is much narrower in scope than what she has previously experienced. This narrowness allows subjects to be studied to a much greater depth, studying one or two subjects thoroughly, rather than many superficially.

As students proceed through the educational system the focus of study tends to get narrower and narrower. First year studies at university might seem quite specialised at first, but in the final year there will be opportunities to investigate very specific areas of the subject in a detail that may not have been examined by anyone else before.

Having said that, in a strange way the boundaries between subjects also become more blurred. Chris may be studying French but some analyses of French language or literature require the use and understanding of sophisticated computing procedures.

She may be studying for a Biology degree, but that may also mean that she will need a good grasp of Mathematics and Chemistry and maybe some Physics. So although she will be focused on one subject she may well have to learn aspects of others to solve basic problems.

The teaching

Good university teaching is not so much about delivering sets of facts or truths, but about exposing students' minds to current ideas about a topic and making them *think*. Many students find it difficult to make the switch from learning facts to evaluating evidence.

Students often ask us, "But how does X really work?", or, "What is the relationship between Y and Z?". Our answers are usually along the lines of "What do you think?", as we attempt to engage the student in debate. We are not ducking the questions asked, and will give our opinion... eventually. Usually there is no stock, or 'correct' answer and many students find this 'woolliness' worrying.

But students should persevere because, at the forefront of knowledge, subjects do have a woolly nature where little is fixed and much is opinion based on available evidence. If in doubt, discuss!

Seminar or tutorial type teaching is very good for stimulating discussion with and between students, but there are many other types of teaching delivery at universities – see Chapter 7 *Teaching*. Whatever type, the onus is firmly on the independent student to make the best of the experience.

School teaching usually involves class sizes under 35 and some scope for individual attention. At A level the class size is normally no more than 20 and often less. While attention to the individual is not by any means lost at universities, do not be surprised to find Chris in very large classes where, understandably, focusing on the needs of a single student is not possible.

How can Chris learn in such an environment? By using her independence to seek solutions. Read about the subject and discuss it! And just how big are these classes? Lectures to in excess of 350 students are not uncommon and neither are practical classes involving over 50 students, especially early on where students from more than one course may take sessions or modules together.

All teaching is necessarily incomplete, though sometimes lecturers forget to tell students this. "Necessarily" because students are expected to be independent learners and use means other than direct teaching, such as books, to understand a topic. Teaching should thus be viewed by students as skeletal: a frame on which to base their understanding of a subject.

One inevitable consequence of what we've just covered is that Chris will have less contact with academic staff than she did with her teachers at school. In some courses formal contact might only amount to a few hours a week. It's a grave error for students to imagine that the rest of the time is for non-academic activities. It's not.

That time is for a student's own study of the subject: it should be used wisely. Remember that Chris will be expected to work for about 40 hours a week on her academic subjects.

Chris's views count

In some types of education the learners sometimes have a say in how they are taught. For example, schools often have a 'student council'. In many cases its purpose is more to do with developing the councillors (the students) and giving them a sense of ownership in their education, rather than it being an effective vehicle for change.

At university, however, Chris's views really will count. Universities need to show that they are taking the opinions of their students seriously. They do this typically by questionnaires where students are asked to rate the module, course or even individual lecturers, and/or by holding regular meetings with students or student representatives – students elected, nominated or cajoled by the students themselves.

So if Chris thinks there is something inappropriate about her studies, encourage her to voice her opinion or to ask her student rep to raise it. We could cite many examples from our own experiences where students have suggested extremely useful changes that have enhanced the learning experience for them.

Students often do not realise that they are the only ones who get to experience the course they are doing. At school or college they may have had the same teacher for the whole of their A level course. That teacher knew everything that went on in the teaching of that subject. At university there may be ten or twenty individual staff members contributing to the degree course. They obviously know the contents of the course in broad outline but few, if any of them, will have experienced it all. Only the students get to see it all and only they can have valid opinions about the overall content of the course including where it may be deficient, repetitive or even contradictory.

So if Chris rings one day railing about incompetent staff telling her contradictory things, then remind her that the staff are not doing it on purpose and that it is her responsibility to advise the staff about the course because she and her colleagues are the only ones to experience the 'whole shebang'.

Sometimes the changes make life easier for the lecturers too. Chris should not be quiet! Remember we said that Chris's employment prospects can be enhanced by little extras? Being a student rep can develop many skills that employers will be interested in.

And finally …

If you're now a little alarmed by just how different university is from school, or indeed perhaps anything else you've experienced, remember that most students, probably including Chris, take the changes experienced as a normal part of passing through the educational system. Chances are, you will be more worried than her.

Parents often worry about 'how it all fits together', that is, how will Chris develop as a person, keeping track of all the things she does and learns? Universities are concerned about this too and 'Personal Development Planning' – the keeping of a record of achievements, aspirations, worries, and skills levels – must now be offered to students.

Actually this description of Personal Development Planning is rather simple, as you'll see in Chapter 11 *What next?*, but the basic idea is that students are aware of the totality of what they have learned and experienced at university, and possibly throughout their lives. This isn't just for CV building; often students don't know that they have acquired a particular skill until they stop to think about it!

There are two things that connect to everything covered in this chapter. One is independence, which we cannot stress enough. The other is perhaps more nebulous: thinking. You could ask a thousand people about the purpose of universities and you might get a thousand answers, but many of the answers would mention 'intellectual' or 'clever' or some other attribute associated with thinking.

One of the most important things to be developed at university is Chris's ability to think rationally, perhaps laterally, and to examine evidence and draw conclusions. We just want to remind you that thinking is pretty important. But you and Chris don't need to enrol in a Thinking class to be good thinkers! Think about it!

Chapter 5

Learning

Learning is, without doubt, a personal business. It's so personal, i.e. it's never the same for any two people, so that even giving professional advice about it is difficult. So what can you do to help? You can appreciate what learning is like at university and that individuals are different in the ways they learn – we'll try to illustrate these things in this chapter.

Just as we are different from each other in how we learn, so you are likely to be different from Chris. There's no rights and wrongs about learning. But by learning about how universities think their students should learn, you'll be in a better position to point Chris in the right direction. Hopefully you will see in this chapter that learning at university is very different from learning at school, or in any other setting come to that.

You might think that there's little advice you could give about learning, and you might be right. But we need you to understand what learning is like at university because it will pervade all Chris does academically when she gets there. You will probably find it difficult to understand the ethos behind the assessment and teaching at university until you understand what university learning is about.

That is why we have put this chapter before those on *Assessment* and *Teaching*. So don't feel a failure if you're not able to advise on learning itself – though we provide some ideas – because by reading this chapter you'll be on a much firmer footing in advising on, and understanding, other academic matters, such as how Chris will be assessed. Read on! You might learn something!

Doesn't learning come with teaching?

Like many academic staff we sometimes act as 'external examiners' at other universities (Chapter 6 *Assessment* gives details of how this system works). In writing an external examiner's report, one of us was asked recently to "*comment on the quality of teaching … methods that may be indicated by student performance*". He replied, "*I find it hard to comment on how the quality of teaching, or anything else for that matter, has contributed to student performance. I imagine that good quality teaching … has led to high quality graduates; but the teaching quality could be terrible and the students extremely well-motivated to give the same effect!*" Get the picture?

Without actually participating in the learning process, it is difficult to understand how that learning took place, especially in a university setting where the learners are encouraged to be 'independent'. We could teach someone for several hours about the structure and function of the human respiratory system, but if that someone spends the whole time looking out of the window, reading, or listening to an iPod, we might as well not have bothered. We have taught, and perhaps taught well, but no one has learned.

Thus teaching and learning are two separate activities and one doesn't necessarily follow the other. This is why we have chosen to separate them in this book. At school a teacher might rightly be admonished if his teaching didn't lead to learning in his pupils, but at university there is not such a strong link. True, if a whole group of students failed, the university would probably ask questions of the lecturer, but there is no defined onus on the lecturer to make sure that his or her students learn.

So when Chris returns to the nest at vacation time and you discover that she has knowledge and understanding of her chosen subject, is that *because* she has experienced good teaching or *despite* her experiencing bad teaching? You can't be sure. But what you can be sure of is that Chris will have matured as a 'learner'.

How to learn at university

Of those students who fail to complete their course of study, by far the majority leave within the first few weeks of the first year. There are, of course, a variety of reasons for this. Many of these reasons are to do with inadequate preparation for what it will be like at university and we hope that the preceding chapter has helped you, and helped you to prepare Chris, in this respect.

Some will leave because they can't adjust to the type of study, and although we can't be sure how many this applies to, we expect it is a significant proportion. For many academic staff, we can presume that their personal experience of school is in the distant past. Further, we can presume that these staff effectively managed the transition from school learning to university learning – or else they wouldn't be teaching at university.

These presumptions lead us to suppose that academics may have forgotten, or be unaware of, how difficult that transition can be. Despite considerable academic support services in universities (see Chapter 8 *Student support services*), many students are not pointed to them or are unaware of them. This can result in students languishing in self-doubt and a failure to make the switch to this business of independent learning.

We certainly don't want Chris to end up in that situation, so let's discuss how learning is achieved at university. Actually let's start by understanding how learning *isn't* achieved.

Getting into university can be a real achievement and there is a temptation to relax – certainly the atmosphere at university is conducive to that in comparison to school – but therein lies the trap. Many students arrive at university and see themselves rather like a sponge, ready to soak up all the teaching that is delivered to them and, given a little squeeze, to spill it all out again when the assessments come around. They're passive, if you like. This is how learning isn't achieved at universities. Students can be forgiven for having this view: it might have worked well for them in the past where all they needed to do was turn up and soak up the teaching, and complete the explicit tasks set for them, perhaps in the form of homework. It's worth revisiting what we said in the last chapter: the onus is firmly on the university student to learn, not on the academic staff to teach.

This is because universities are about producing graduates who can compete as independent individuals on the world stage. Universities do not produce robots who can regurgitate material fed into them – a bit like schools do – but produce individuals who can use their inherent and learned skills to exploit a given situation to full effect.

So independence and a shift of responsibility from the teacher to the learner are the cornerstones of a university education. Students who don't realise this are in for a shock and may never complete their course. Make sure Chris is aware: universities may assume too much of their entrants.

Of course academic staff will guide Chris through the things she needs to be aware of and may help by giving specific pointers to learning and to assessment. They will take the horse, Chris, to water, but they cannot and will not force her to drink one single drop. So if Chris is confused about how to learn, she should ask and discuss this with one of her lecturers.

Interestingly, while learning at university prepares students for the 'world of work' – indeed it is argued by some that such preparation is the function of learning and teaching at universities – learning at work is different. The working environment tends to consist of goals to be achieved, targets to be met, and a focus on the particular job at hand. Learning at work is often termed 'training' or 'staff development', though this isn't to say that employees can't learn from all aspects of their jobs.

University learning is different in that it offers a chance to explore, to enquire, and is a real opportunity to 'broaden one's mind'. This is certainly what it did for us and we are confident that it will be true for Chris too.

But what should she learn and how should she learn at university? She should be resourceful. And this is where you come in and can have a real positive impact. Let's deal with the 'what' first.

She should find out as much as possible about that 'what': information can come from course handbooks, module guides, lectures and face-to-face or e-mail discussions with lecturers. She should then have a firm grasp of the subject matter, and, if not, she should ask again. She shouldn't make the mistake of leaving her learning until an assessment crops up: she should be prepared.

Armed with the 'what' she can then tackle the 'how'. As a first point she should make sure that she understands the material she has been taught in lectures, practical classes, seminars, etc. One way to do this is to re-write the notes she took in every session, cross referencing them with textbooks which should be available in the university library, the titles of which should have been indicated to her, probably in a module guide.

In the later stages of a course, textbooks may not be sufficient – they take too long to produce to be of much use in investigating research topics – and so the original research articles or reports should be consulted, which again can be accessed via the library or through the internet. She should be generally wary, however, of sources of information on the internet because they may not be reliable (see Chapter 6 *Assessment*).

Once she is confident in obtaining information in this way to support her studies she will be well on the way to becoming an independent learner, deciding for herself, as her 'learning confidence' matures, which supplementary material found in this way is important for inclusion and which is not. When she comes across material in books or research articles that is contradictory she should seek advice from a lecturer.

Most lecturers love to help students who have shown some degree of independence already. The ability and confidence to discuss topics with academic staff is itself a sign of maturity and independence and will be welcomed.

Remember we said Chris should be resourceful? Where's the place for resources at a university? The library. These days libraries may be re-named 'information centres', 'learning resource centres' or somesuch, which might be better terms describing what they provide. No matter. Every university library is a wonderful resource. Chris should make sure she knows how to use and exploit it.

It's also important to effectively combine the 'what' and the 'how'. We remember a student who fell in love with the university library. He was in awe of the vast array of materials he could access, particularly textbooks. He was studying Economics and would go to the library to check out a few economic reports and forecasts and emerge six hours later having read a book on Renaissance Painting.

Needless to say he didn't pass his assessments. But he was an independent learner. He had the 'how' but somehow the 'what' passed him by. Perhaps his problem lay in his choice of subject to study, more about which in Chapter 10 *Avoiding and recovering from a poor start*.

You can help Chris by returning again and again to her subject matter and reminding her about the pointers to the 'what' of learning issued by academic staff, for example in a module guide. Try to ensure she's learning the right things. It's the prerogative of a parent to nag!

But, it needn't be a nag ... just simply ask Chris what's she been reading recently and take it from there. Who knows ... you might learn something as well! One of us, trained originally as a botanist, learned a whole load of psychology from an offspring in this way.

Self-assessment of learning

For many students, it is important to consolidate learning by trying to estimate what it is that they have learned. Again you can help here, whether Chris is having difficulty or not, by getting her, at regular intervals, say once per term, to list on the left-hand side of a page the skills and understanding that she has gained thus far in her university career. Shy away from 'facts' she might know, just concentrate on the skills and understanding bits.

Then on the right-hand side get her to indicate how she learned the items she listed on the left. In this way both you and she can keep a check on what she is learning and how she is learning. If the items on the right of the page don't seem to indicate that she is moving towards independence (as a worst case scenario all that is listed is 'lectures') then you might like to gently nudge her towards more independent means of learning.

We mention skills here because these are important too. For example, "working with others in a team" might not be something Chris has acknowledged. But she might have developed, even mastered, that skill, though without alerting her to it, she might never realise that she possesses it. This 'learning audit' is not only good for confidence building, but provides items to enhance a CV (see Chapter 11 *What next?*).

Also, the ability to recognise one's own achievements and, hopefully as a consequence, the gaps in one's understanding or skills is an important one to develop that will help Chris in her university career and beyond. So don't shy away: try to get involved.

Perhaps produce your own list and share it with Chris: get her to be critical about your learning – you don't have to be at university to learn! In this way, coming together as peers you might find a better channel of communication. We're not suggesting this works for everyone, but suck it and see!

Actually, awareness of their own learning is something that universities try to get students to achieve through the Personal Development Planning process, more of which in Chapter 11 *What next?*

More on independence

We've all served our time on appointment panels for academic staff at our own and other universities. These days we are guided in our choice of successful candidates by 'person specifications' and 'job descriptions'.

Universities are rightly interested in getting good teachers on their staff, but they are concerned with other things too, such as the research record, or potential, of applicants. Besides, if teaching is to be led by research, where the boundaries of knowledge are pushed back, it makes sense to have active researchers among the academic staff.

Some people are superb researchers and are also able to communicate their findings and those of others in an effective manner to undergraduates. These are the people universities want to appoint. But this combination of skills isn't common and so there has to be a balance.

While it's generally accepted that academic staff will engage in research *and* teaching, it's only natural that some are better at one than the other. Furthermore, some staff might be employed solely to teach and others solely to conduct research, with the latter perhaps contributing to research-led teaching such as is found towards the end of a degree course, for example in supervising research projects or research dissertations.

What we're trying to say is that some staff might be more approachable, accessible and useful to undergraduates than others and that this is the natural way in which universities operate (more about this in Chapter 7 *Teaching*). On top of this there is the notion that all academic staff do is teach and that they enjoy luxurious long holidays when the students aren't around.

Nothing could be further from the truth (well we would say that, wouldn't we?): universities still function out of term time. Academic staff are usually very busy all of the time. Even in vacations there is pressure on them to keep pace with their subject, do research, publish the results, disseminate the results at conferences, bring in external funding for their research, and cope with a mountain of administrative material.

What we're trying to say now is that staff have enormous pressures on their time and teaching and engaging with undergraduates can only be one of them. Such is, and always has been, the reality of universities.

What's the purpose of our mini-essay above on the woes of an academic? For Chris, all the above means that independence is more important than perhaps we've indicated before. With the best will in the world, academic staff cannot be there all the time for every student. Sometimes she might not be able to get a response from staff when she needs help – she needs to be prepared for this, and be prepared to seek her own solutions.

There's no magic formula to being independent in learning, Chris will just have to be resourceful. Again, if all else fails, use the library. Apart from making Chris aware of the above, there's a role for you too. That is in providing unequivocal support. If she knows you are there to help and to suggest alternatives, that might be half the battle won. Persevere with Chris and try to be involved in what she's doing, if only by telephone or computer.

CASE STUDY – PHILIPPE

Philippe excelled at A levels. He was passionate about history and had an amazing memory for facts. He was accepted to study Modern History at his first choice of university, some 100 miles from his parental home. Although he found socialising with other students difficult, this didn't deter him from his studies. Quite the opposite in fact, and he worked hard to do well, partly to please his parents who had high expectations of him.

He was keen to please academic staff too and tried to impress them with his knowledge of history. In turn, the academic staff found Philippe diligent and always willing to listen and to participate in discussions. He became particularly friendly with one professor, probably because the professor was willing to listen to Philippe's ideas and to engage him in debate. But the professor was concerned about some of Philippe's ideas and the notion that Philippe seemed fascinated by popular and sensationalist 'facts' that were at best on the margins of the course.

Philippe would ask, "So who do you think shot Kennedy?", or, "Is Elvis really dead? I read an article that said he wasn't". Within two months of entering university the first assessment loomed. It was part of a module run by the professor, a multiple choice test that covered the material delivered to Philippe in lectures, material Philippe was expected to find out about for himself from textbooks, and contained some questions to test understanding and the ability to evaluate evidence.

Unfortunately Philippe failed the test. Given the interest Philippe had shown in history, the professor examined Philippe's answers and found that he had done well on those questions that covered the material that was directly taught, showed limited understanding of the topic and limited ability to weigh up the pros and cons of an argument, but failed to get a single question correct that covered material Philippe was supposed to find out about for himself. The professor called Philippe in to have a chat.

The professor indicated the importance of wider reading of the subject to Philippe's studies and suggested where Philippe might start. Philippe tried to listen but was rather pre-occupied with a news item he'd recently read about a hoard of Second World War gold that had been discovered off Scotland. Philippe knew that he should read more textbooks, but found the sheer number of them daunting and, even despite the professor's 'sign-posting', didn't really know how far he should read into a subject at first year level.

Philippe took the test again and failed again. Worse, he also failed many of his other modules for the same reason. As we write this, Philippe is taking a year out from university, deciding whether to return.

He could have stayed on, his failures weren't irretrievable, but at that point he felt that university learning wasn't for him. Philippe is staying in the city where the university is: much though he loves his parents, he prefers not to go home where he thinks his failure will be seen as a disappointment.

In short, Philippe hadn't learned how to learn at university. Philippe was right in that university learning just isn't right for some people, but it might have been 'right' for him under different circumstances. Universities offer all sorts of help (see Chapter 8 *Student support services*) that Philippe could have accessed once he recognised that he had a problem – certainly after he failed the multiple choice test twice.

Most universities offer workbooks, short courses or drop-in sessions on how to learn and usually these are advertised during induction. He could and should have focused on the requirements of the course and modules: these should have been clearly laid out and, if not, he should have asked.

You could argue that the professor should have offered more help, perhaps directing Philippe to the appropriate university service.But professors are busy juggling a raft of university roles and may not be able to spot a specific weakness that warrants a specific remedy: unless they're psychology professors, professors aren't psychologists!

If Chris looks like becoming a Philippe, do try to rationalise with her and get her to focus on what it is that is being asked of her at university. Learning to learn isn't easy for some and pointing her in the right direction could be a big, perhaps crucial, help.

There's another point here, too. We guess that Philippe didn't want to talk issues over with his parents, which is a great shame. While you obviously want Chris to do well (otherwise you wouldn't be reading this book), it's important to cajole and support the decisions Chris makes, rather than imposing high expectations on her. 'Parent pressure' can sometimes have devastating results and may have contributed to Philippe's early departure from university.

Thinking

Somebody once said that universities exist to teach people how to think. We would probably agree that that is part of what universities do, but what is meant by 'thinking'? As well as learning about subjects at university, students use their subjects as vehicles for learning various skills that could be placed under the banner of 'thinking'.

We're referring to the ability to evaluate evidence and come to a logical conclusion; to solve problems; to sift through information in order to prioritise what is relevant to a problem; to be critical of opinions, actions and motivations, and to be critical of oneself; to be able to present a logical and developing argument; to synthesise information from different sources in order to address a problem; and similar intellectual skills.

Universities take their role in the development of these skills very seriously and as Chris progresses through her course you should be able to see a change in the way in which she expresses opinions, tackles problems, etc. If you're in doubt about this, the next time she expresses a point of view ask her what evidence she has used to form that opinion.

We've tested this on our long-suffering children and friends' children and found that they are usually pretty woolly about assembling evidence and rationalising it before they go to university, but once there they seem to get better and better. Try it! If nothing else it will let you know that Chris is learning something of value.

Thinking embodies a group of skills that are vital for research, as well as most other pursuits and activities at an advanced level, from railway timetabling to plumbing. Ultimately research is about finding out about something, asking questions, and perhaps testing one's own ideas along the way. Most university lecturers engage in some sort of research and that may be why they are good at fostering thinking skills in their students.

Two pearls of wisdom are rapidly realised by those who are engaged in research. The first is how little we humans actually know about the real world. The second is that any 'fact' is only as good as the evidence that supports it. In short, we don't know much and we question what we do know. Final year students in Honours degree courses come to know these pearls as they get a taste of research. But without that experience of research, the pearls can be difficult to grasp.

Universities may not directly relate this to students, but you can to Chris. As Chris starts at university, whatever her prior study, things in her accumulated knowledge will be fixed – the things she, you and we call 'facts'. To university academic staff, facts are very hard to pin down and everything is open to question.

Consequently, staff can be very vague in answering even the simplest question and this can be a real turn-off for students who may think that staff are being deliberately evasive. They're not. They're merely adopting a professional academic stance and in doing so are trying to encourage their students to do the same. The emphasis is more on fostering debate. To academics most topics are in development, unclear, probably not well researched and perhaps controversial.

Academics give the best answer they can, given that a large part of their job is about thinking and the promotion of thinking skills. Mind you, academics can get understandably dismayed if they're asked about information the students already have or can easily find out for themselves. Again, students may not be forewarned of what to expect, but you can 'warn' Chris. The most rapid way for Chris to integrate into our academic community is for her to join in: do some thinking of her own and question what the lecturers have to say. They'll always welcome a thinker!

Why all this fuss about learning and thinking?

Universities are sometimes ridiculed for offering degrees in so-called "Mickey Mouse" subjects; things like Football Studies or Adventure Travel. Outside the strictly vocational degrees such as Medicine or Law, the subject of a degree, however, could be considered as the vehicle a group of academic staff use to develop in their students the graduate thinking skills we've been discussing.

Employers look for evidence of these thinking skills. In that sense the study of History or Physics is just as irrelevant to employment as is Golf Management. What *is* important is that graduates have developed independence and can come to reasoned judgements; in short that they can think.

Getting you to think about this and to pass those thoughts on to Chris is a valuable first step in opening Chris's mind to the way universities operate in educating students – or should that be the way universities operate in allowing students to educate themselves? Universities are under an obligation to teach students how to think: even if they wanted to, universities couldn't just teach facts.

This is because the UK, through the Frameworks for Higher Education Qualifications (available from the QAA at *www.qaa.ac.uk*: click on 'Academic Infrastructure'), stipulates what the holder of a degree should be able to demonstrate. For example, in England, Wales and Northern Ireland, holders of Honours degrees should be able to:

- devise and sustain arguments;
- solve problems;
- comment on particular aspects of current research;
- appreciate the uncertainty, ambiguity and limits of knowledge;
- manage their own learning;
- critically evaluate arguments, assumptions, abstract concepts and data to make judgements;
- show decision-making in complex and unpredictable contexts.

The list above constitutes just a few examples we've picked out. The version for Scotland is slightly different, but it retains the ethos behind the elements above. Note that "manage their own learning" is in there. In Scotland it gets an even bigger mention as, "systematically identify and address their own learning needs". We hope that by now you can see why we and universities take independence, learning and thinking so seriously.

So if Chris wonders why the things she's learning seem so woolly or why she has to manage her own learning, you can tell her not only is it good for her, but that it's enshrined in the nation's policies!

And finally …

Please think again about what we said at the beginning of this chapter. While we have described the elements of learning at university, learning is a very personal business. We want to emphasise that no matter how much help you provide, learning is a very personal business. Do we need to say it again? OK then, we will.

We handle the teaching. We handle the assessments. We handle the awarding of degrees. The learning is handled by Chris.

Chapter 6

Assessment

The assessment system

During Chris's years at university she will be set a series of tasks so that academic staff can make judgements about whether her work meets the standards required for her particular degree course.

She will always be told when and how her performance is being assessed. Except for examinations, she will usually be told how she might have performed the task to an even higher standard. So, what do you know about the assessment system in universities and how can you help Chris to survive the system?

Universities are assessment organisations; the only thing that students cannot do for themselves is to assess their own work (though there are peer-assessment schemes in some courses where students mark each other's work and, in order to develop a student's critical faculties, they *are* sometimes asked to assess their own work). Students learn for themselves and the teaching could be seen as just providing the structure for the learning to take place ... and that just leaves the assessment ...

You need to understand how assessment works at university; and if you went to university more than ten years ago, you can forget what you think you know because the assessment landscape has changed radically.

Two things often come as a surprise to some parents. The first is that most universities have the legal power to determine who is worthy of their awards. In practice this means that university staff mark assessments and, in general, they are not sent away to be marked by outside bodies, such as examination boards. This means that the lecturer who teaches a class also sets and marks the assessment. There is a safeguard in the external examining system where one or more 'experts' from other universities also examine the assessed work, especially later in courses, to ensure everything is fair.

The second is that assessments cannot be re-taken to improve a mark, unlike in some other systems, such as UK A levels. Though schemes vary between universities and individual courses, typically Chris will get two opportunities to pass each assessment. If the assessment is not passed at the first attempt then one more attempt is allowed but the maximum mark she can then get is a bare pass (typically 40%).

Also, the second attempt might not involve exactly the same assessment task – something that can catch out the unwary student – though it will probably test the same skills, knowledge and understanding.

There is, and probably has always been, a fundamental difference in assessment between schools and universities. The UK A level or Scottish Highers curriculum that drives the teaching and assessment in UK schools is a detailed set of instructions to an *examining* team. The curriculum contains *all* that a student is required to know and do. The examiners are instructed not to stray outside the boundaries set by the written specification. Thus it is possible to pass by knowing less than is specified – and most students do! The examinations 'sample' the specified curriculum since it is not possible to test it all.

At university, the 'curriculum', is called a 'programme specification' and is mainly a list of outcomes and a list of module contents, and it represents the *minimum* specification. It contains what every student needs to be able to do in order to pass *at a minimum level*. Thus, there is an expectation that the assessment will test ALL the key outcomes. To do well in the university system a student should be looking to know more and do better than that which is specified.

We operate like this for two reasons. First, we have an expectation that eventually some of our students will know more than we do. To restrict the curriculum would be to say to students, "It is not worth doing that because you will not get any credit for it", thus stifling the independence we are keen to promote.

Second, the specification is a sort of contract between us and the students and between us and future employers. It says that anyone who graduates with this degree will be able to do all these things and we know they can do them because they have performed these sorts of tasks to an appropriate standard – we have tested the students through assessment.

Learning outcomes – it's all about the end point

In practice, courses and modules have learning outcomes and although in reality students pay little attention to these, they are the key to understanding how the assessment system works. They're also relatively new.

Let's look at a familiar example, the driving test. The examiner has a checklist for the test – these are the learning outcomes. The assessment of driving ability will address these learning outcomes and will cover ALL of them. In a driving test the examiner doesn't choose four areas out of six to test you on … all successful candidates have to demonstrate competence in ALL the learning outcomes, but the examiner has discretion in *how* you are assessed against each outcome. For example, manoeuvring the car can be assessed by parking, turning in the road, etc.

And so it is with courses and modules in universities. Each module will have its own set of learning outcomes and the assessment for that module will focus on determining how well Chris has achieved *all* those learning outcomes. They are thus of fundamental importance and Chris will ignore them at her peril. Each assessment element will be cross-referenced to the learning outcomes. It's certainly worth emphasising these when talking to Chris about assessment.

Does Chris know what the learning outcomes are for a particular module? In preparing an assignment, maybe a practical report, did she look through the learning outcomes to make sure that these were being met by her report? Make sure Chris is aware that the curriculum is only a minimum specification. Like a driving test, a pass simply signifies that the candidate has reached the minimum specification and can now drive independently – it makes no statement about being a good or even an average driver.

As students progress through the university system, there are subtle changes in the way learning outcomes are written and thus what the examiners are looking for in a student's work. At level 1 – the first year in a full-time degree scheme – learning outcomes will be written using terms such as

- Describe, Recall, Show, Identify, List, State,

while at level 3 (typically the final year) the emphasis may change and words such as

- Synthesise, Criticise, Evaluate, Integrate, Generalise, Justify,

find their way into learning outcomes.

Similarly, many learning outcomes specify not just subject-based knowledge, but also the skills that should have been acquired (or enhanced) during the progress of the module. Thus it would not be exceptional to see learning outcomes framed something like:

Having passed this module a student, (say in Underwater Basket Weaving), *will be able to:*

a. Recall the facts and principles of underwater basket weaving using 'green' willow twigs;

b. Design a basket;

c. Construct a basket; and

d. Give an illustrated talk on an aspect of underwater basket weaving.

Note that these learning outcomes do not state how well these tasks have to be performed.

An assessment might be worded as:

Prepare and give an illustrated talk on the topic: Underwater basket weaving – the advantages of 'green' willow twigs over other easily obtainable twigs (to address learning outcomes a and d).

Assessment criteria – how Chris's work will be assessed

Another big change in student assessment has been the introduction of assessment criteria. These are not 'the answers'! Remember, Chris may well be working and learning in areas of the subject in which there are no 'right' answers anyway. The assessment criteria, usually issued to students in advance of the work, describe the qualities of work worthy of particular grades. One criterion might be the quality of the writing and include a statement such as:

Outstanding, well-directed presentation, logically and coherently structured, using correct grammar, spelling and reference citation

in describing work worthy of a high mark, and

Inadequate presentation, structure, grammar, spelling and reference citation

as the characteristics of a fail.

These criteria operate, therefore, as guidelines to what the staff expect within a piece of coursework, how marks will be allocated and what characteristics a good answer might have. This should provide a 'blue-print' for a piece of work and should not be dismissed lightly and certainly not ignored. Again, it is well worth alerting Chris to these and checking with her that she understands them.

We stressed earlier that we want Chris to be an independent learner. But you can see from this that there is plenty of advice about what she will have to do and how well she will have to do it. She should be in no doubt about the quality of work expected; and, if she is, then all she has to do is ask for the assessment criteria. And if she doesn't understand them, then ... ask for advice.

Practical help – what you can do

Nowadays, nearly all students will have two basic forms of assessment, written examinations and coursework, sometimes called cumulative assessment or continuous assessment (it is not actually continuous – but Chris may think it seems like that!). Students like Chris can get very 'up-tight' about written examinations.

In the first year this is partly due to the fear of the unknown – she may not have had to sit a three-hour written exam before. That in itself can be daunting and it is quite a leap from exams lasting one and a half hours to ones lasting twice as long. Reassurance is a great help: "You can do it!" But practical help is always a bonus, so two important points worth making to Chris are as follows.

1. Get a revision timetable organised and STICK TO IT. Make sure the timetable isn't too taxing – leave space for a social life, taking the iPod for a long walk, doing the washing, watching *EastEnders*. It has to be realistic. Many students leave things too late and therefore have to give up everything in order to concentrate on revision work; with the end result that

the quality of revision that comes with 'little and often' cannot be achieved. The result is 'shallow' learning (i.e. just knowing the 'facts') and that's not what universities are looking for. 'Deep' learning (i.e. understanding and the ability to synthesise ideas, etc.) should be the goal and that comes from immersion and dedication.

2.   Vary revision strategies. Revision is not just about reading and trying to remember; quality revision comes from active engagement with the subject – making notes, creating 'mind-maps', designing mnemonics, practising answers within time limits. Make it interesting; make it varied.

And, if Chris is actually around the house during revision time, you can observe this behaviour at first hand. If it seems that she is 'holed-up' and in a 'rut' the answer is easy – suggest a trip to HMV for some retail therapy or a trip to the local cinema or golf driving range or whatever it is that turns Chris on. Three hours of solid revision isn't good for anyone.

Coursework – how to maximise Chris's chances

There is now a huge variety of different coursework assessment tasks and it is impossible to generalise on these but some points may help when Chris phones for advice.

Coursework is nearly always set early in a module. Assessments such as essays, reports, literature reviews are given well in advance of deadlines and usually there is nothing to stop Chris starting – and finishing – these well before the due date. Nevertheless, Chris and her friends may well be found in the computer room typing up assignments at 2 o'clock on the morning of the due date.

Experience has taught us that the common feature that all successful students have, regardless of any other characteristics, is good time-management skills.

One of us remembers asking his son once a week what the workload was like and whether he had assignments due and when he was planning to do them. Such enquiries may be seen as intrusive or nagging ... it just depends how you approach the subject. And you can always recount your own disasters of poor time-management while at university/work/organising your own wedding, etc.

Students do get stressed about coursework assessments. It's a myth to believe that the coming of coursework has lightened the stress-factor on students. It hasn't – it's just spread the stress. Be prepared therefore for Chris to be anxious throughout the term. It's usually not something to be alarmed at but hints of stress in Chris's behaviour are often rooted in a looming coursework submission deadline.

Coursework is like most tasks. It may seem enormous when viewed as a whole but cutting it up into bite-sized chunks will make it more manageable. And the chunks do not have to be done all at the same time. Discuss with her the wisdom of planning something and then leaving it for a while. When she comes back to it, it will be familiar and, therefore, more manageable. She may also see the flaws in it.

Students get very upset at having to give presentations or 'talks' – it's one of the constant criticisms that students make of modules that have a presentation as part of the coursework. Many courses allow students to practise before giving a presentation and often presentations are delivered to small tutorial groups before being given to the whole class. Nevertheless, students do get 'stressed-out'. Courses insist on this particular 'graduate skill' because verbal communication is an important skill in the work place and is often written into job specifications as 'essential'.

Chris needs to know that practice does make perfect – or at least acceptable – and that is the message to convey. If possible, offer to hear her presentation. She may be a bit self-conscious but the discussion afterwards is extremely useful. In professional life we often practise talks in front of our colleagues. Criticism is a part of life and leads to improvement; and understanding how to take criticism is a 'graduate skill' in itself.

When academics mark students' work, they sometimes go to extraordinary lengths to point out to the students what the good points of the work were, where there were weaknesses in the work and what could be done in the future to improve similar assignments. This 'feedback' is regarded by academic staff as an important point of contact with students, and an integral component of the dialogue between them, not to be disregarded.

If Chris is on a course where there is little contact with academic staff, then this indirect contact is even more important. Feedback might be better thought of as 'feed-forward' because it gives very valuable advice on how Chris might improve in the future. Emphasise to Chris just how important feed-forward is in helping students to improve. Often students are much more preoccupied with the mark awarded than the feed-forward. This is a pity because usually the feed-forward is much more important to their learning.

So, if Chris has done rather poorly in a piece of work, ask her what the comments were on the work and talk these through with her. And, if she needs further advice and clarification, encourage her to ask her tutor. This won't be seen as pestering or a weakness but will be seen as a keen student willing to learn from her mistakes and hoping to do better next time. You wouldn't want to fail a driving test without some guidance on what you did wrong and what you should do to improve before taking the next test.

Occasionally Chris will get work back with a mark and no comments. This could be a lazy lecturer but more likely the lecturer has given some generic feedback. That is, most of the work marked had similar strengths and weaknesses and, rather than write out the same comments on each piece of work, there will be a single comments sheet available. But still, if Chris requires more feedback, she should ask for it; encourage her to ask!

Know the assessment system

Of course, Chris might miss an assessment or deadline, or be prevented from performing to the best of her abilities because of illness or a personal reason. If this is the case, Chris should make sure the university is aware of her circumstances as soon as she can. She should contact the person who set the assessment for advice.

All universities have systems in place to help students in this situation: she should use them. Many universities will want to see some sort of evidence that Chris was genuinely unable to perform. If she has a personal problem it might be worthwhile seeking out the counselling service so that a counsellor will be able to support her case (see Chapter 8 *Student support services*). The counselling might help too!

Many universities assume that if a student is so ill as to prevent attendance, the student will be so ill that a doctor should be consulted. This isn't unreasonable and the doctor will be able to provide Chris with a note that she can give to the university to explain her absence or less than top-notch performance.

If Chris fails an assignment, it's not the end of the world and the failure has to be put into perspective … a role for you. Chris, if she is a conscientious student, will be devastated at failing an assignment, particularly if she has made it through GCSEs and A levels or Highers with little upset. However, one failure does not make for a failed student. Encouragement is essential.

Try to find out if Chris really knows why the work failed. Are there sufficient feed-forward comments to enable Chris to understand the shortcomings of the work? If not, encourage her to go and find out. And when she has, talk through how this might help her improve in the future.

Failure in one component does not usually mean failure of the whole module. This is a gross generalisation, but for many modules at years one and two there will be one examination worth between about 40-60% and coursework will make up the balance. The coursework marks will probably be divided between approximately two to four separate assignments – Chris may be able to afford to fail a component without failing the module. But check – sometimes all components must be passed in order to pass the module.

Failure in examinations is more difficult to cope with. In most cases it will entail a retake or re-sit, but not always! If the failure is not particularly bad and there is meritorious work in other modules, then the failure might be 'condoned' or 'compensated'.

If not, apart from the extra stress that this puts on Chris, it might also upset summer plans as re-sit examinations are often not held until mid- to late-August or even until September. The trip to Florida may have to be put on hold or the summer job worked around revision – and note that it shouldn't be the other way round!

Additionally, feed-forward is not usually given on examinations, though there does appear to be a move in Higher Education for students to be given supervised access to their scripts in order that they can see where they went wrong. The difficulty is that staff are not obliged to annotate examination scripts to the same degree as coursework and also do not add the same type of helpful comments.

Therefore, if Chris is able to see her script, then she has to work to see where the deficiencies lie. But, it's worth doing. If viewing the script is not illuminating, then encourage Chris to talk to the tutor in charge – ask for advice on revision, advice on suitable textbooks to support revision, advice on how to approach particular question types, and so on … and you should be able to help here as well. She should ask and discuss!

It's also worthwhile to take a little time to understand the scheduling of Chris's assessments. Many universities, but not all, operate two semesters per year, one from September/October to January/February and one from then until May/June. All teaching and assessment may be contained within the semesters, so Chris *may* have two sets of exams per year.

For some universities 'referral' is the term used to describe less than a pass mark for a piece of coursework, an exam or a module, but there is an opportunity to re-sit to achieve a bare pass; and 'deferral' means that a pass mark has not been achieved but that some unusual circumstances, such as illness, may account for this and there is an opportunity to sit the assessment again with the full range of marks available. Usually an assessment or examination board will meet to consider student achievement shortly after the examinations period and its conclusions will be transmitted to Chris. This could mean after each semester, or only in June, and probably again after re-sits in September. You should find out which system applies to the course Chris is studying. We provide this information because we know of one student (not one of ours) who managed to persuade his parents that he was progressing normally, but because we knew the pattern of examinations and assessments it was clear to us that he was having to do several re-sits.

The consequences of failure in one or more modules become more severe the further Chris is into her university career. Many universities will allow Chris to make up the module she has failed in her subsequent year – but be wary of this because Chris now has an extra load and it will be worth pointing this out, perhaps suggesting that, if permissible, she takes the module as 'stand alone' and resumes her studies a year later. This will, of course, mean a delay in graduation, but might prevent the award of a poor degree.

Also, be sure to find out how the final degree result is calculated. Some universities and courses measure the 'exit velocity' of their students, taking some average of Chris's final year results. Others want to ensure that students are working hard earlier in their university career and so may include second year and perhaps even first year results in the calculation too. Check – this will obviously influence Chris's approach to study! Let's give you an example.

CASE STUDY – MARK AND ALAN

Mark and Alan met because they both answered an advert for rooms in a shared house. They got on instantly, largely thanks to having the same taste in music. They were both in their second year at the same university; Mark was studying Biology and Alan, Electronics. They were both interested in science and technology in general and spent much time talking about popular science, either in their shared house or, more likely, in bars.

Such was their passion that both intended to continue their studies after graduation by working towards PhDs. They also spent much time going to gigs together and with a wider group of friends. Though they had girlfriends, travelling to and enjoying live music was a large part of their lives.

Of the two, Mark was slightly more gregarious and encouraged Alan to take his studies less seriously than perhaps he should have.

With late nights spent completing coursework and judicious swotting for exams, both managed to scrape a pass and were able to continue their studies into the final year. Mark knew that only his final year counted towards his overall mark, intended to pull out all the stops for that final year, and assumed this was the same for all courses at all universities.

Unfortunately the situation wasn't the same for Alan. Although Alan's university department had told him that 50 % of the overall marks came from the second year, this information was lost in all the other information issued to him and probably lay in a carrier bag under his bed. Both Alan and Mark found the final year difficult, largely because they hadn't prepared themselves well, but they worked hard.

Both achieved a similar set of results for that year, but Mark graduated with an upper second class degree and Alan a lower second, simply because of the difference in the way the overall mark was calculated in their respective departments. Mark went on to complete a PhD, but because of his lower classification, Alan did not. Although Alan went on to a sponsored training scheme with a large communications firm and is now a senior executive, he still regrets not being able to do a PhD.

So be sure to find out how Chris's final degree result is calculated, though we most certainly don't recommend Mark's strategy! There's another lesson here too: universities issue a lot of information and usually it is important: Chris shouldn't 'lose' any of it, especially when it concerns assessment.

P.S. Mark admits to being pretty lazy during his first two years at university, knowing full well that only the final year 'counted'. With hindsight he recognises that this was not the best way to guarantee success in the final year. In fact, had he concentrated on his studies more he would probably have emerged from university with a higher class of degree. We know Mark well: he's one of us! So sustained effort is important too. Make sure Chris knows this.

Using sources of information in assessed work

Isn't the internet a great resource? All that information available and so accessible. Just a few key words and you will usually find what you want. But how do you know that what you are reading on the internet is true? The fact is, you don't. And neither do students.

As they progress through university, students come to realise that the internet is not such a great thing after all and they switch from taking information from it uncritically, to using it to search for information that is likely to be true. The difference? Consider an academic textbook. To get the attention of a publisher in the first place the authors usually have strong professional records in their chosen field. Before publication the manuscript is reviewed by other experts in the field to verify the contents. After publication the book might be reviewed in specialist journals that focus on the subject.

Compare that to a website: even those with a limited knowledge of computing can produce a web page or two and there is no check on the accuracy of its contents. Often our students quote material from what they think are reputable sites, or confuse opinion with fact because of the way information is presented on the internet. One student once wrote an essay on "The origin of life" based on one university professor's internet site.

Unfortunately for the student that professor was a radical and his ideas were illogical. But the student didn't realise this. Others use on-line encyclopaedias, not realising that literally anyone can post information there. There really is no substitute for the textbook. These days, many textbooks come with a CD-ROM that allows students to access good information by electronic means, should using a computer be important to them. As students mature they use the internet usefully to search for electronic copies of journal articles, or data from government or industry websites.

The internet *is* great, so long as it is used with thought. The message here? If your Chris is a rampant user of the internet you might like to remind her that it takes a lot of time to know which sites to trust. If you are sceptical about newspapers, you should be even more sceptical about the internet. Good advice is to use the university library: that's a great resource too.

... and a pitfall to avoid

It's also worth making sure that Chris understands the university's rules on plagiarism – passing off the work and ideas of others as your own. You might be horrified to think that Chris would do this, but it's an easy trap to fall into. Consider the student who was set a task to find out about a topic and give her views on it. She went to the library and searched the internet and found a reputable source of information. She then presented that information unchanged as part of her report. This is very easy from electronic sources of information with 'cut and paste' technology.

When the work was marked she discovered she had scored zero and worse, was being investigated for a breach of the regulations! This is not an uncommon scenario. Unwittingly she had passed someone else's work off as her own and was guilty of plagiarism.

Universities take plagiarism very seriously indeed, as appropriate preparation for professional life where copying someone else's work unacknowledged is a definite no-no: consider issues over 'sampling' in the music industry. Universities now have the means to detect plagiarism through electronic searches on phrases in students' work and there is software specifically designed to do this.

Universities draw the attention of students to the pitfalls of plagiarism, but this is often buried in other material. Consider advising Chris that whereas at school the finding and inclusion of other's material in assessed work might have been appropriate, it is expressly forbidden at university.

Chris should know that if she must directly quote someone else's work, for literary purposes for example, then it's essential that she indicates that it is a quotation and gives a citation, such as 'Darwin (1859)' in the text and a full reference to the book, article or (reputable) internet site later in a 'References' section.

If she finds information of value to her work, it should be paraphrased – put into her own words – before including it in work to be assessed. But again remind her that she should cite the original source in the text and list the reference in the References section.

Plagiarism is ventriloquism – someone else speaking through the mouths of our students. We are not interested in that. We are interested in what Chris knows and can do, and from where she learned these things.

And finally …

So, is there a general message about assessment? Academics are not in the business of failing students. Indeed, if student failure or withdrawal rates increase, alarm bells start to ring and strategies are put into place to attempt to reverse the trend. Further, academic staff do not like to fail students and will do their utmost to ensure that students who have the ability to progress really do progress. However, it is, and has to be, a two-way process. Chris has to make the effort through her independence.

If coursework or examinations are failed it is up to Chris to be proactive about seeking advice – though most staff would also have in place mechanisms to help even the most recalcitrant student. Encourage Chris to talk to her tutors and encourage her to do so when everything is still fresh in her mind. And, follow that up a few days later by asking how the meeting went and what strategies Chris has now developed in order to get over the hurdle. Ask and discuss!

Chapter 7

Teaching

If you're dipping into this book and have dipped straight to this Chapter to find out what university teaching is about, you've probably made the wrong move. We strongly suggest that you read Chapter 5 on *Learning* first. It's the learning that's important: the teaching is merely one of many vehicles that can help students to learn. Universities are learning-focused, but learning is the business of students. This apparent paradox was explained in Chapter 5.

Teaching is what we, as academic staff, do. We organise teaching sessions that are designed to help Chris to learn. We are also trying to produce independent learners, so the support we provide might not be as immediate as it was at school or college (see Chapter 5 *Learning*) and we tend to teach about the questions rather than the answers. Most of all, Chris needs to be prepared for the change from the type of teaching she experienced at school or college.

Of the three Chapters on academic life at university (Chapters 5, 6 and 7) we've put this one last because you have the least direct influence here and because the others are simply more important: learning is paramount, and assessment tests that learning has taken place. Once Chris realises that learning is something that she has to manage, she will come to view the teaching and various teaching sessions at university as opportunities to help her in her primary focus – to learn.

Teaching then shouldn't be viewed as a chore along the lines of "oh no, not another 9 o'clock lecture", but as a chance to both demonstrate and enhance learning. By "demonstrate learning" we mean to interact with the teaching staff and other students.

To ask and discuss. This is not to say we're suggesting Chris behaves like a 'swot', constantly interrupting to demonstrate her own abilities and knowledge; what we are suggesting is to question and inquire as appropriate.

Chris will soon get to know what "appropriate" means relative to each teaching session. But what she shouldn't be is silent. Silent students scare us. This is because we don't know whether they're engaged with the material we are teaching or not. Chris should be vocal and use the teaching to help her to learn.

Differences between school or college and university

An obvious but rarely stated difference between school or college and university is freedom: the freedom that comes with the independence we've been discussing. One of our daughters is in the sixth form at school, studying for A levels. She has to be present at 8.55 every morning, regardless of when her first lesson is, which sometimes means she has two hours of what the school calls 'private study' before lessons begin.

She has to wear a school uniform, including a tie. She is not allowed to wear jewellery or make-up and is not allowed to dye her hair. She is not allowed to leave school premises, even at lunch time to visit the chip shop/pizza parlour across the lane. It's all a bit restrictive for her and in stark contrast to one of her friends who has set up home with a partner and just had a baby. It seems that she's old enough for some things but not for others.

One of our sons is also studying for A levels, but at a further education college and there are none of these restrictions placed on him. Consequently he is, to some extent, managing his own learning in that he has to manage his own timetable, and this might mean an easier transition into university for him.

What we are trying to illustrate is that this transition can be easier for some than for others because of what they have done immediately before going to university.

What you can do is make Chris aware that restrictions, if any, will be gone, and that by and large she will have to decide what to do, when to do it, and how to get to where she needs to be. You might think Chris won't need such reminding, and you know Chris best, but we see lots of students who find it difficult to cope with the freedom – a lack of instructions, if you like – foist upon them when they enter university.

These students appear to us like lost sheep, and though we try to help where we can, we can't be there for all of them all the time, nor would we want to be.

Some of our 'lost sheep' seem to like sleeping. We don't see them for days. While attendance at school was rigorously enforced through the use of registers, at university the practices vary. When we run a teaching session, it is solely for the benefit of our students; thus we expect them to attend, even though there may be no compulsion.

For some courses there may be no attendance requirement at all – the position in most courses over ten years ago – for others all sessions may be compulsory, and for others only those sessions where students must demonstrate a particular skill, or are assessed in some other way, may be compulsory. Chris should find out what the attendance requirements for her course are.

Although a diligent Chris will want to attend all sessions, the reality may be somewhat different and the consequences of her actions should be known to her. Even where attendance is not compulsory she may be missed and this might trigger a mini-investigation by her personal tutor.

If Chris's attendance is poor, a letter – addressed to Chris, of course – may be sent both to her term-time address and her permanent address (assuming the two are different) suggesting that she pulls her socks up. If letters do arrive from the university, see if Chris is willing to discuss their contents with you. A softly, softly approach is recommended because we often find that poor attendance is the tip of some underlying problem that has not yet been raised with the university's support services (see Chapter 8 *Student support services*). However, there may be a much simpler cause: in our experience the most likely are too many late nights and too much paid employment.

In Chapter 5 *Learning* we mentioned that academic staff might not be appointed by universities on the basis of their ability to teach. Often appointment is on the basis of their abilities as an all-rounder in teaching, research and administration. Consequently, while almost everyone who taught Chris at school has a qualification in teaching, many of her lecturers at university will not.

Almost all universities require new members of academic staff who have little teaching experience to study for a qualification in university teaching. These courses are often concerned with the educational theory or the 'ethos' behind good teaching and may not place as much emphasis on day-to-day teaching skills as you might think. Nevertheless, this doesn't mean that all younger staff are 'good' teachers and all us older staff just somehow muddle through.

As it is at school, there will be staff who are good at teaching and those who are, well, less good. If Chris is having difficulty understanding what she should be learning from a specific member of staff, she should ask and discuss, as opposed to forgetting about it until the gap in her learning is exposed by an assessment.

A university won't be too sympathetic if a student complains about the quality of teaching *after* the assessment, having done nothing to raise the university's awareness *before* the assessment. Talk to a personal tutor, talk to whoever runs the module or the course; but talk to someone!

A perennial complaint from students is that staff are difficult to find. This is true. When not in their offices, staff might be teaching somewhere; at a conference; on research leave; at home writing a book; doing research in the library, a laboratory, or up the Orinoco; at a university meeting on any subject you care to name; with a colleague grappling with the intricacies of timetabling; acting as a consultant to big or small businesses, etc., etc.

In trying to find our colleagues *we* are often frustrated; students are in the same boat. We know of many students who have tried, and failed, to find us. They may have repeatedly returned to our offices and had the misfortune to repeatedly find us absent. Some have been known to sit on the floor in the corridor as though they were waiting for a January sale, camping out all day when we were having an all-day meeting trying to decide who should write which bits of this book.

So what's the solution? Students should do what we do. First, plan ahead. Make sure that the issue isn't burning, i.e. it can wait a few days. Second, do not despair: other means of contact are available. Put a note under the office door. Seek out a secretary or personal assistant who may be able to relay a message.

Perhaps the best remedy is to send an e-mail. That way there's hard evidence of the attempt to make contact. Some staff are aware of their necessary shortcomings in the availability stakes and indicate their 'surgery hours' to students, times when they will be available for consultation.

So if Chris tells you of difficulty in making contact with staff, you know a little about how those staff organise (or disorganise) their time and you might have some useful suggestions at hand.

Even more on independence

We won't expect Chris to be a fully-formed independent learner when she arrives with us, but we will expect this when she leaves us. There will be a gradual change in the way we teach her which will match, drive even, the move towards independence. At first there might be a lot of factual material (knowledge) for Chris to soak up, along with some leanings towards developing her own arguments.

Later in the course there may be less 'factual' instruction and more debate on contemporary theories about topics. What's happening is the curriculum is switching from being about what we as humans think we know (knowledge-led) to being about how to find things out (research-led).

The switch may happen without Chris knowing about it. You can check that it is taking place by asking Chris for the *details*, if she lets you, of what it is that she is learning. You should notice a switch from facts to non-facts – unknowns, opinions, theories. If by the time she reaches her final year Chris isn't showing that her learning is about evidence and how to gather and assess it, then you might want to probe this a little further, perhaps bearing in mind the qualities expected in graduates that we mentioned at the end of Chapter 5 *Learning*.

There's also a switch in the resources Chris will use to aid her learning and you can check this too. Textbooks are good tools early in Chris's university career, but they tend to be 'factsy' in structure. In the later stages of courses the learning is based around topics that are unclear or are evolving.

As a result, textbooks quickly become out of date and don't help much at the cutting edge. Students and staff therefore rely much more heavily on research articles and reports, which are able to keep pace with current developments in a field. So in her final year

Chris should be accessing reports of research. Is she? Can she list the main sources she uses?

Why does this switch occur anyway? Apart from the fact that it's always been there, we again turn to the Frameworks for Higher Education Qualifications that formalise it. For Honours degrees in England, Wales and Northern Ireland, the Framework asks for "an understanding of a complex body of knowledge, some of it at the current boundaries of an academic discipline" and an "ability... to make use of specialist reviews and primary [i.e. research] sources".

Also, remember we said that staff might be recruited for their research profile? Many staff will be using their research findings in their teaching, especially in the final years of an Honours degree. All Honours degree students get a chance to demonstrate that they can do research of their own, typically through a project, dissertation or performance. The Framework again stipulates this as the "ability to deploy accurately established techniques of analysis and enquiry". The Framework for Scotland is identical in sentiment. So Chris should be forming her own opinions within her chosen subject – this is a good check for you that she's learning the right things and learning to learn for herself.

The teaching itself

TEACHING SESSIONS

If the average person is asked how students are taught at university, the answer is likely to involve the word 'lecture'. But lectures are only one means by which the course content is delivered to students. So expect Chris to experience a range of delivery types – there are lots of them, too many to detail here, but if you want some examples then there are seminars, tutorials, discussion groups, problem-solving classes, field trips, practical classes, performance work and workshops.

Also, Chris can expect a variety of approaches to each type of teaching delivery. As an example, let's stick to the lecture. It could be an uninterrupted long talk about a topic, with or without illustrations. Sometimes the illustrations or indeed the entire talk are supplied as hand-outs or through some electronic means, sometimes not. It may be broken up by asking students to think or participate at various points, or students might be asked to fill in 'missing' sections in hand-outs as the lecture progresses or through reading after the class has finished. You get the idea: approaches vary.

Whatever the approach, it is very important that Chris leaves the formal teaching session with a good understanding of the main points presented. To help with this she'll need to take notes.

NOTE-TAKING

There is a variety of books available on this subject and some universities even produce their own guides, so we are not going to give specific advice. But we are going to give general advice: Chris should make sure she has a record of what happened in each teaching session. She should take notes during every taught session, or if this is not practicable, make notes immediately afterwards while the material is fresh in her mind.

She shouldn't be shy of recording in writing her experience of practical classes or practice-based work as it happens: all students find it hard to recall details later. A good aim would be to make sufficient records to be able to describe in full what happened to someone who wasn't there.

In lectures this may mean making notes as she goes along. Inevitably there will be bits she does not understand and it will be important to note these down so that she can follow them up later, either by reading books, discussing it with friends, or seeking advice from staff. She will need to act as a filter for the information she is presented with and decide which to retain for future reference. She shouldn't make the mistake of assuming that only what the lecturer writes down is important: some of the verbal material is key too!

One of us once experimented with students by communicating an important point verbally in a lecture. No student wrote it down. But when "I would like a large ice-cream" was written on an overhead transparency, all the students copied it down. Chris should be independent in lectures too! Oh, and Chris should know what to do if she is unsure about note-taking: ask and discuss it! Note-taking is important.

You could ask Chris about her experiences and so help develop her skills here. If she finds it difficult then encourage her to practise – news reports, chat shows, documentaries on TV and radio are all suitable though the speed may be a little faster than the average lecture. Do it with her and compare what she got out of a broadcast with what you noted down.

THE TIMETABLE

Chris's timetable might be skeletal. In some arts courses we might be talking about three to four hours a week that are formally timetabled, and you already know that the rest of the time is for Chris to get to grips with her chosen subject. You can probably see that time spent in the presence of academic staff is at a premium, so Chris shouldn't waste such opportunities.

If Chris is living at your home and you think she doesn't seem to be spending much time at university, try to find out why – likewise if she lives at university but comes home for extended weekends.

Deadlines for assessments are often set weeks and perhaps months in advance. A sustained effort is needed. Many assignments are designed so that they require such sustained effort and this will show through in good presentation and a mature approach; last-minute work will be slip-shod by comparison and will attract few marks. Push Chris for continued work – to keep her eye on the ball.

WHO DOES THE TEACHING?

In many universities there is much pressure on staff to do research. This is good for Chris because it exposes her to staff with ideas at the forefront of her chosen discipline. The downside is that academic staff have less time available for teaching. One way in which almost all universities address this problem is to bring in other staff to teach part of the curriculum. This can be beneficial for students when part-time or 'visiting' lecturers are used because they often have roles in the wider world that can positively influence their teaching.

Consider training in elements of general practice in medicine. Who would be best to teach Chris? An academic who hasn't seen a patient in 30 years or a currently practising GP? What about developing characters in 21st century novels? Who's best: an academic who's never published a novel or someone whose latest book was a critical triumph?

The use of 'visiting' lecturers can enhance almost any academic course. In their teaching programmes universities may also make use of their own research staff or students studying for higher degrees such as a doctorate. Many universities call these people 'graduate teaching assistants', or GTAs.

These folk don't often lecture but may contribute to other teaching such as running practical, seminar or tutorial classes. These opportunities to interact with people just a little further on in their understanding of a subject might be invaluable for Chris. Opportunities for research staff to gain teaching experience are generally viewed as valuable by all concerned and may help them to decide if a career in a university is suitable for them. If Chris has aspirations in research, she can look forward to this opportunity too.

So if your routine enquiries as to what university is like for Chris reveal that she's being taught by non-academic staff, don't let the alarm bells ring. Only let them ring if Chris is having a poor experience, regardless of who is doing the teaching. One problem is that non-academic staff are rarely available for consultation outside their formal teaching hours.

So if Chris has problems with the subject material then she will need to collar the lecturer immediately after the teaching session. If she continues to have problems then she should have a word with her student rep (see Chapter 4 *What it's like at university*), her tutor or whoever is in charge of her course.

One of the consequences of having teaching delivered by research-focused academic staff is that some of the material might be controversial. One of us remembers being taught some very controversial stuff at university. Unfortunately, the lecturer failed to indicate that the material was his personal pet theory, at odds with the collective wisdom of all other experts in that field on the planet.

Luckily for Chris, the controversial material doesn't usually rear its head until the later stages of a course, by which time she should be sceptical about what the lecturer has to say and be able to verify it, or not, by reference to research articles. So don't be surprised if Chris comes out with some wacky ideas – test and probe them and see if a 'maverick' lecturer is involved. In this sense 'maverick' doesn't mean wrong or even inappropriate. It's good for students to be exposed to new ideas. In fact lecturers are often encouraged to present these ideas to undergraduates in an attempt to stimulate them into thinking and in order to get feedback from sharp minds.

CASE STUDY – MOHAMMED

Mohammed wanted passionately to be a social worker, following in his uncle's footsteps. He could trace his passion to the time his uncle let a wide-eyed 12-year-old accompany him to a conference on social integration. Mohammed studied for Highers in Scotland and did astonishingly well. To say Mohammed was focused would have been putting it mildly.

He coupled his drive with an enormous amount of excitement as he entered university to study for a three-year B.A. Honours degree in Social Work. In his first year he excelled. His tutors regarded him as a patient and thoughtful individual who would be able to sympathise with his future clients.

Like his Highers, the degree course was modular. Mohammed successfully tackled the various elements of his course as taught *in* the modules but, though he didn't know it, he never really got to grips with the 'big picture', being able to integrate what he had learned *across* the modules.

This wasn't really Mohammed's fault: the modules and their assessments were self-contained, almost forcing him to think in boxes without connections between them and so it was easy for Mohammed to 'tick-off' each particular subject as he studied it. The second year was different.

Here the course adopted a different stance that, while still composed of modules, took a problem-based learning approach. In essence, students in groups were supplied with a set of case studies and developed means of progressing the cases, solving problems of social, legal and moral dimensions along the way. Students also had to prepare and present an oral report.

This approach to teaching required two things that Mohammed wasn't prepared for: working with other students and doing some 'joined-up thinking' to solve problems. The problem-based approach was signalled in the prospectus and course handbook, but Mohammed had paid little attention to it.

In short Mohammed didn't like working as part of a team – or giving a talk – and regarded the other students at worst as lazy and at best as piggy-backing on his knowledge. Mohammed scraped through the second year, and completed his degree, but his experiences disillusioned him to the extent that he's now working (happily) as a resource planner in the social policy section of a county council. Mohammed's story is one of success, but not in what he set out to achieve.

What can we, you and Chris learn from Mohammed's experiences? Apart from making sure that the course's delivery fits in with the way Chris wants to learn, three points arise. First, remember that a problem-based approach is now used in many courses, in part to simulate the real world that graduates will be operating in. Some students find it difficult to integrate what they have learned from their various modules and bring that learning to bear to tackle a problem.

If Chris finds herself on such a course you can support her by getting her to ask, in advance, for some examples of problem-based learning so that she can be prepared.

Second, the compartmentalisation of learning can be dangerous, students missing the 'big picture'. Perhaps encourage Chris to make connections between her various modules and remind her that what she does in one module might be designed to prepare her for what is to come in another.

Third, team work is an important skill for a graduate to have and so Chris should expect to have some exposure to it, whether she likes it or not. Further, just as real world teams succeed or fail as a group, Chris should expect to have some assessments at the level of the group, i.e. all members of the group get the same mark no matter what their contribution.

This might seem unfair, but it does reflect real life. Many problems in the real world are solved not by members of a single profession, but by teams who have representatives of many professions, or in jargon, multi-professional teams. Getting some experience in this at university could be invaluable and is certainly good fodder for the CV.

Finally, remember that it is not reasonable to expect Chris, or anyone else, to be good at everything. She will have strengths and weaknesses. She will be able to exploit her strengths in some parts of the course, but other parts may expose some weaknesses. This does not mean she is not doing her best, but it might mean that she will have to adapt rapidly to new ways of working. Support her when her weaknesses have been exposed.

And finally ...

If Chris doesn't understand the point of what she's being taught, i.e. why she's learning it, it's probably worth discussing in detail with her the material and how it's taught. Not everything Chris learns will be directly and explicitly linked to her academic subject.

The material that Chris is concerned about may well be more to do with developing Chris as an independent learner than bolstering her knowledge of underwater basket weaving. We again refer to the Frameworks for Higher Education Qualifications, which essentially list the skills that all graduates should have. Communicating information is clearly flagged up and teamwork, though not explicitly mentioned, is implicit in many of the other skills listed.

So be supportive when Chris asks why she must give a talk in front of the class, and remember that, when she starts her first job, what she *knows* will be much less important than what she can *do*. This is where you can come to the fore.

You might struggle in helping her with the finer points of quantum mechanics or the reasons for the Russian revolution, but you can help in honing Chris's graduate skills, largely skills of 'thinking' (see Chapter 5 *Learning*) and communication. For more on these see Chapter 11 *What next?*

Chapter 8

Student support services

As parents you can provide much needed encouragement and support for Chris during the early weeks of her course and indeed throughout her time at university. Contact can be established by phone, text-message, e-mail, internet messaging services, or even by snail-mail.

Establish and maintain contact by whatever means is convenient and be there for her when she needs you. Remember that the human voice is a great comfort and more efficient than text-messaging or e-mail, even if it is more expensive. But you can't be there for her all the time and if Chris is at university in Exeter and you live in Aberdeen, then she can't just nip home for a comforting chat and a hug.

Besides which, sometimes more than a comforting chat is needed. Students supporting each other – peer-support – is a marvellous thing and they will 'look out' for each other but, again, sometimes the support that is required is above and beyond what friends can supply. But don't worry because the university village is self-sustaining and looks after its own.

Even the smallest institutions will have over a thousand students all of whom are potentially vulnerable individuals. And it is no surprise that all universities have a formalised student support network in place to help students professionally, should it be necessary.

The vast majority of students never need to access student support services, but for those that do, a warm, friendly, helpful and professional welcome is guaranteed. Our personal experience suggests that these are the most dedicated staff within universities and nothing seems to be too much trouble. This chapter then is about raising your awareness of the professional help available, including that from the academic staff themselves.

The professionals

So, what do student support services offer? This will vary from university to university and if Chris has any specific difficulties that she needs help with then it is worth checking things out before application. For example, if Chris has a disability it is worth alerting the universities that she is hoping to apply to in order that investigations can begin into what adjustments might have to be made to accommodate Chris's needs (see section on *Disability services*).

In this chapter we list what's likely to be available and nowadays the range of advice and support is extensive. For example, one university runs a 'Well-being Centre' with drop-in services for health, mental health, 'lifestyle' as well as booked services for relaxation, smoking cessation, health MOT, fitness and lifestyle evaluation, and on issues such as motivation, confidence and self-esteem.

The same university also offers a range of complementary approaches, for example, aromatherapy, homeopathy, dietary analysis, reflexology and Indian head massage. We obviously can't go into all of these, but we do cover the main bases here.

The counselling service – there to help

Earlier in this book we emphasised that starting university is a very traumatic experience. One student told us that those first few days of teaching were the worst of his life and that he lived in a state of panic not knowing whether to 'stick it out' or to take the next train home and back to the nest. He was one of the fortunate ones – he stuck it out and succeeded.

Statistics tell us that the majority of students who drop out of university do so in the first term of their first year and that the majority of those leave after only the first few weeks – and we have already outlined many strategies that you, as a parent, can use to help Chris through the tough times. But, when you can't be there, there are professional helpers and these are to be found in the counselling service of the university. If you think Chris is likely to use the service it might be worth checking out the counselling website of prospective universities.

Counsellors are good helpers because they don't have a vested interest in the problems students face and won't push students to the counsellor's preferred solution. It's about helping students to reach the best decision for themselves. Simply being listened to can be of enormous benefit.

What's more, the counsellors are professionals – they've been trained for their role. And it's a confidential service, so don't think Chris's counsellor will discuss Chris's situation with you. Don't even ask! In exceptional circumstances Chris's counsellor may contact you, but only when this is in Chris's best interest and then only with Chris's permission.

Universities want their students to succeed and counselling services help achieve that goal. In fact, counselling could be the key factor that enables Chris to complete her course of study, as it is with a number of students. Chris shouldn't be afraid to use them. Let's face it, we all have problems!

Referrals to the counselling service can come from a variety of sources. Friends can advise Chris that she really ought to see a counsellor, or her academic or personal tutor might *advise* (but never *instruct*) that course of action. Or it may come from you. Or Chris may self-refer. If you are a long distance from Chris you might want her to put herself into the hands of dedicated professionals who will make sure that she gets the very best advice.

There is no stigma attached to this. The very last thing that a university wants is for students to suffer or fail because they don't get proper and timely advice. If you feel Chris's stress levels are rising, make sure that you discuss with Chris the possibilities of seeking help. She'll thank you for it in the long run.

Healthcare provision

Universities may provide healthcare for their students through dedicated medical centres. But not all do, especially the smaller universities. So if on-going health care is important to Chris, and therefore to you, the facilities should be checked out prior to application. If Chris is living away from home she should register with a local GP, but if there's an on-campus medical facility this will provide much practical advice as well.

The advice is focused on the demands of their relatively young clientele; you would probably find few flyers on Alzheimer's in the waiting room of your average university medical centre. Some of the advice relates directly to the needs of university students, for example examination stress and how it may be dealt with.

Other advice relates to the needs of young folk anywhere – on the effects of smoking, alcohol and substance abuse, the importance of exercise, weight control and diet, HIV testing and counselling on contraception and pregnancy, preventative medicine such as cervical smears, vaccinations, and on specific medical conditions such as raised blood pressure, asthma, diabetes, meningitis, epilepsy, etc.

These are professional services run by professionals for aspiring professionals, and the quality of provision is excellent. You can rest assured that if Chris has to engage with the medical services on campus she will be well looked after.

CASE STUDY – JASMINE

Jasmine was a first year student studying French and Politics at a large city-based university. She appeared to be a very friendly, happy-go-lucky student and within a few weeks had acquired a circle of very close friends. They worked together and played together and Jasmine seemed to have made a successful transition into Higher Education.

In telephone calls home she told her mum how happy she was and how quickly she had settled in. But Jasmine's tutor (she had a tutorial once a week with three other students) had noticed that she always seemed very subdued in tutorials, even lethargic.

She also noticed that Jasmine was very thin: not skeletal but definitely underweight. Half-way through the semester, Jasmine failed to turn up for her weekly tutorial. Her tutor made enquiries and found Jasmine had been feeling unwell for several days.

She had collapsed while out with her friends and, after a number of very long heart-to-heart sessions, they finally persuaded her to see one of the staff at the university health centre. She took one of her new friends with her for the appointment.

It transpired that she had not eaten for over a week and anorexia, which she had developed while studying for her GCSEs, had returned. At this stage she was quite seriously ill and the university doctor arranged for her to be admitted to hospital where she remained for nearly two months. Her friends and tutors kept in touch and visited regularly but it was clear that she couldn't complete her course at that stage. She took a leave of absence and was told that she could rejoin her course when she was fit.

The counselling service at the university arranged for specialist support during and after her stay in hospital. By spring she was much improved and had started to put on weight; her mum was a tower of strength as she had suffered a similar illness during her younger years. Her university friends, too, were very supportive.

Finally, nearly one year later, she re-joined her course as a first year student. Her second year friends are still very close and still 'look out' for her and she keeps in touch with her counsellors. Peer and parental support and a professional health and counselling service helped save Jasmine's life.

Such support is common-place in the university village. It was perhaps a pity that this medical condition was not declared to the university as it might have been possible to offer support at a very early stage and before things became serious.

Jasmine's is, of course, an extreme case. But if there's a medical condition or a disability that might affect Chris's study, it should be declared. The university will be supportive and Chris can concentrate better on her studies.

Disability services

If Chris has a disability you are probably already familiar through experience at school level with the services that are currently in place to support students. In universities there has been a substantial change in recent years and this change has been driven by legislation.

In the UK (except Northern Ireland) the appropriate legislation is the *Special Educational Needs and Disability Act 2001 (SENDA)* while in Northern Ireland it is through the *Special Educational Needs and Disability (Northern Ireland) Order 2005 (SENDO)* that amended the *Disability Discrimination Act (1995) (DDA)* and became Part IV of that Act.

This legislation applies to all the activities and services that a university provides either wholly or mainly for its students, from the very first contact at open days or on the receipt of information on courses, in prospectuses perhaps, through to graduation. It protects all students from discrimination, including disabled students, disabled applicants and disabled prospective students.

The legislation has caused institutions to re-evaluate their provision and support for disabled students in Higher Education. Before the Act/Order any adjustments that were made were driven by university policies or advice from the Higher Education Funding Council for England or by the influence of the Quality Assurance Agency's *Code of practice, Section 3, Students with Disabilities*. Chapter 12 *Other sources of information* gives details.

Much consisted of ad-hoc adjustments and arrangements. Now, the landscape is created by the concept of 'reasonable adjustments', i.e. that the university should take reasonable steps to ensure disabled students are not placed at a 'substantial' disadvantage in any aspect of university life. This, of course, includes admissions, enrolments, assessments and examinations, adapting the curriculum or the mode of delivery, providing additional services such as sign language interpreters, as well as alterations to the physical environment.

Universities are alerted to a disabled student's needs when they receive the UCAS form because applicants are able to include a 'flag' indicating a disability – this should trigger a response and most universities will have a protocol that swings into action in order to fully assess the needs of the prospective student even at this very early stage.

Between 1994-5 and 2005-6 the percentage of disabled first year UK domiciled students rose from 3.11 to 6.38 and the needs of students with disabilities are well-catered for, though there is still much to do. If you have any concerns at all about the level of support that Chris might expect, contact the university student support services. You will find them extremely helpful. Support mechanisms are becoming more commonplace and sophisticated and you will be astonished at what is on offer. Chris shouldn't be tempted to hide her disability from the university. Undeclared disabilities cause problems for the university and for the student.

Universities want students to succeed whatever their disability, and are required to and will help students to complete their courses of study. So don't be put off if Chris has a disability. In 2005 there were 45,425 disabled students in their first year at UK universities and good examples are provided by blind students in the UK and the USA who have successfully completed degrees in Medicine.

Of course Chris may not have any disabilities at the time of application but may be diagnosed with a disability after joining an institution.

Despite the work done in schools, we are still diagnosing students with dyslexia at university and a significant number of such students are 'found' each year. In many ways, this is a testament to the support mechanisms that are in place, for example allowing students to take self-diagnosing computer tests before formal diagnosis with an educational psychologist.

Thus you can rest assured that if Chris is found to have a disability while at university she will have the full support of student services.

If you wish to find out more about supporting students with disabilities you should visit the website of Skill, the National Bureau for Students with Disabilities (*www.skill.org.uk*). The 'Disability Discrimination Code of Practice for Further & Higher Education' (*www.equalityni.org/archive/pdf/DDisFHEAppCOP0106.pdf*) published by the Equality Commission for Northern Ireland contains a wide range of practical examples and the adjustments that should be made, and this may well give you confidence in what you might expect for Chris.

Childcare services – please be quiet so that mummy can finish this essay

If Chris has a child (or children) then congratulations grand-daddy/grand-mummy! The good news is that just about all universities offer childcare facilities. These are typically open to the children of both staff and students – who often get reduced rates – and, sometimes, to children whose parents have no formal links with the university.

As universities are diversity-aware institutions, university childcare facilities will also usually cater for children who have special needs or who are disabled. They typically have a mission to develop babies, toddlers and children rather than just providing a 'baby-sitting' service.

It's important to talk things through with Chris even before application just to make sure that the facilities are in place and the small-print has been scrutinised. For example, you and Chris might want to know: how late the facility stays open; whether there is coverage during the holiday periods; if Chris will have to take the baby/child out at lunchtimes or if Chris junior can be left there all day; etc.

Accommodation – a roof over one's head

Many universities require all (or many) first year students to live in university-owned or university-controlled residences. Often friendships made there lead to flat/house-sharing in subsequent years and these friendships may well develop into life-long relationships. But the university accommodation service is more than just about providing on-campus halls of residence accommodation. It will help with finding off-campus accommodation as well as approving rented accommodation.

That is not to say that all university-approved accommodation is perfect – but it will be value for money and conform to health and safety regulations. This book isn't a 'good accommodation guide', but again if palatial living is important to Chris – or perhaps a fast internet connection available 24/7 – then encourage her to check out the accommodation on offer carefully before signing up to a binding legal document that locks her into a contract for the whole year. Your own experience may help here!

The disability service works closely with the accommodation service to ensure that adapted accommodation is available if it is required. Usually universities will have some pre-adapted accommodation in halls of residences suitable for students with disabilities.

If Chris has very special requirements with regard to accommodation then the message is very clear: make early enquiries. If in any doubt, visit the university's website and if your query isn't answered there, then e-mail or telephone one of the contacts.

Financial services – money, money, money

Most universities have some form of independent financial service for students. With the introduction of 'top-up' fees and bursaries, student loans and all the other changes taking place to personal financing, it is often very difficult for a student to be fully aware of what is available and how to benefit from the system. As a parent, it is not always possible to be fully on top of this and professional independent help is appreciated.

The advice offered is focused towards the demands of students, and help is available on a range of financial issues such as state benefits including income support, the disabled students' allowance, housing benefit, general budgetary control, and grappling with the Student Loan Company, grant-awarding bodies or local authorities.

From a parental point of view, the service may also offer information on trust funds. Oh, and if Chris is skint there may be opportunities for obtaining a grant or loan to tide her over. But you and Chris will never know until you ask.

Gizza job – more money, money, money

One of the measures of a university's success is the employment rate of its graduates. Consequently most universities will have an enthusiastic and professional careers advisory service. This can not only help with finding post-graduation employment, but also with summer vacation employment in professional areas, as well as with work-experience placements ranging from a few weeks to a whole year.

So if Chris needs some careers advice, encourage her to make early and regular contact with the university's careers service. The services offered range from help with preparing CVs and filling in application forms to advice on interview techniques, assessment centres, psychometric testing and so on.

The help is practical and focused. You have a role too, in bringing 'life' experiences to discussions with Chris about possible career pathways and that really is invaluable. Nevertheless, life experiences must be balanced with realistic unbiased professional advice, and that is where the careers service can *complement* your input. We'll explore the role of the careers service further in Chapter 11 *What next?*

Academic help

We might have given the impression that university student support services are only reactive to students' needs but nothing could be further from the truth. Yes, they are there when students need them but they also anticipate students' needs, particularly where help with academic matters is concerned. For example, universities routinely run sessions on examination stress and how to handle it, study skills and how to acquire and enhance them, etc.

Familiar sights on many university campuses are drop-in centres where students can get advice on literacy skills (writing, grammar, spelling, punctuation, report writing, essay writing and so on) or numeracy and, often, other skills.

Such support is often available directly from the academic staff as well. For example, take examinations. We've already discussed the differences between exams taken prior to university (A levels, Highers, and such like) and university examinations. Exam preparation is often an important aspect of tutorials with academic staff (particularly in the first term of the first year) and this may involve special sessions where students prepare exam answers to specimen questions; these are then discussed in detail and good and bad points highlighted. After all, it's not in the university's best interest for students to fail.

Indeed, proactive student support is an integral part of an academic's job. Nearly all students are allocated a tutor (sometimes called an advisor of studies, or private or personal tutor); the role of such tutors is to help with academic affairs (e.g. module choice, feedback following examinations, and so on), but often tutors also have a pastoral role. In this, they generally 'look out' for their students and may be proactive in referring students (with their permission) for professional help if it is felt necessary.

Chris will almost certainly be allocated a tutor to 'look out' for her. General problems with learning at university, or indeed anything that might be affecting Chris's ability to succeed at university should be raised with her tutor. If you suspect there's a problem but Chris is reluctant to discuss it, you know where to point her.

And finally ...

If you have specific queries that need to be answered prior to application or at any critical event, check out the Student Support section of the relevant university website – or give them a call. You will find them extremely helpful and very professional. So, what with you and this load of professionals behind Chris, she can hardly fail!

The majority of students never use the student support services. Perhaps they don't know what they're missing! The services are provided for Chris – she should be aware of them and not be afraid of using them.

Chapter 9

Money

So far in this book we've provided you with general help in supporting Chris at university. In many ways, Chris's background, her qualifications, her chosen university and her chosen degree course don't greatly affect how you can provide support.

However, when it comes to money the story is very different. We don't know whether you are 'well-heeled', with the mortgage paid off, a swimming pool of Olympic proportions in the back garden and two Porsches sitting in the drive, or living in a council flat in a deprived area, with water cascading down the bedroom walls when it rains heavily and wishing the council would remove the burnt-out cars littering the 'so-called' car park at the back.

Financial support for Chris in this latter set of circumstances would be very different from that in the former. Because backgrounds vary we can't be too specific. Neither can we be too specific about costs or the schemes available to support Chris because both will change so quickly, the latter with political will. So the approach we've taken here is to provide you with the basic information about costs and where external support is available should you need it.

We've also highlighted a number of useful sources of information that carry things a little further in Chapter 12 *Other sources of information*. Finally, we've tried to provide a balanced picture of the financial pros and cons of going to university. We'd argue that going to university is definitely worth the money, but we've tried to present the facts so that you and Chris can decide for yourselves.

How much will it cost?

Let's assume that Chris is a traditional student (18 years old, single, no kids) living away from home.

First the good news: there are no longer any 'up-front' fees payable for university entrance; the only expenditure prior to going to university nowadays are those associated with preparing for life away from the parental 'nest', the sorts of things we mentioned in Chapter 3 *Student timeline: at university and beyond.*

In Chapter 3 we also mentioned costs while at university, but don't forget the expenditure associated with the specific course that Chris has signed up for. This might include laboratory coats, art materials, musical instruments, field course fees, etc. There might also be costs associated with extra-curricular activities (hockey-sticks, mouth guards, scrum caps, jock-straps, whatever). And there's always the cost of text books – these can be pricier than you might think.

If we assume that Chris has never lived independently and that this will be her first attempt to budget for herself, the best advice you can offer her is in working out a budget well before she even starts packing.

Sit her down and get her to list every conceivable item of expenditure that she is likely to have. Rent … how much is it going to cost and does it include utilities such as electricity, gas, water and telephone? Is there a deposit to pay on her accommodation and how much will it be? What is the likelihood that she will be able to get it back at the end of the letting? What will she need to spend on food each week? Make sure that she tries to estimate how long things will last – how long does it take to get through a kitchen roll or a roll of toilet paper?

Make sure she is aware that while bulk-buying saves money, 24 cans of baked beans take up a lot of space in a cramped student food cupboard. Get her to find out the cost of getting to university from where she will be living. Bus or train or a bicycle? Are there any season tickets or student rates she can take advantage of? Are these in any way restrictive? Can she travel late at night on her ticket if she needs to stay late working in the computer suite? How long does it take to walk? Walking might save money but it might expose Chris to risks that neither she nor you would be happy with. What are the set books for the course and how much do they cost? Are there cheaper sources other than high street stores? Can they be obtained over the internet? Does the Students' Union run a second-hand book stall? Will an earlier edition be OK?

And so on. It's quite a salutary exercise and it really does focus the little grey cells on what the expenditures are likely to be and, importantly, where economies can be made. It may seem tedious and unnecessarily detailed, but the more you can do now to avoid nasty surprises later, the easier it will be for Chris.

Financial help for all

And now we come to fees – are they value for money? It's difficult to know exactly how much it costs a university to educate an average undergraduate – there are too many imponderables. The type of course (there is a very large difference between the costs of educating an English Literature student compared with an Engineer, for example), student:staff ratios, staff salary profiles and so on make it virtually impossible to come up with a sensible figure.

One indication is that the cost to overseas students who have to pay the full cost of tuition is in the region of £8,000 per year. One thing is for sure, therefore: the *actual* cost of educating Chris at university is much more than the tuition fees that she is being asked to pay and so, in one sense, she is getting a very good deal.

The situation with regards to fees is not helped by the fact that there are four jurisdictions setting fees in the UK: England, Wales, Scotland and Northern Ireland; and in Scotland there is a differential fee set for medical courses. The differences between these are explained on the Department for Children, Schools and Families website (*www.dfes.gov.uk*) and this is worth a visit to help you through the minefield.

For the majority of students the fees at a maximum will be just over the £3,000 per annum mark (though again this differs in Scotland) and it is likely that this will only rise in line with inflation. The good news is that Chris doesn't have to find these fees immediately. Instead, Chris will be able to take out a loan (Student Loan for Fees), which is paid directly to the university.

The bad news is that, at some stage in the future, Chris will have to repay this loan but only after she has left university and only after she starts to earn more than a set amount, typically £15-20,000 per annum. Repayments will generally be small, for example a graduate earning £18,000 will only be paying about £5.30 per week.

The level of repayments will depend on Chris's income, not on the size of the loan … more good news for Chris. And the final piece of good news is that the amount repayable will be roughly the same as the amount borrowed, with inflation taken into account. For more up-to-date and precise information you should check the website of Student Finance Direct (*www.studentsupportdirect.co.uk*) – this has links to the support available wherever you are in the UK.

Help is also at hand in the form of grants and loans for general living expenses but these are means-tested – the level of your household income will determine the level of support. Again see Student Finance Direct for current information.

The amounts available vary according to whether Chris will be living at home (in which case they would be lower) or, for example, living in university accommodation in London (in which case they would be higher). So long as the application is made early enough – over to you – payments are made at the start of each term and this will help Chris in budgeting.

A maintenance grant is 'free-money' and doesn't have to be paid back, though the student loan for maintenance does, but, as with the tuition fees, this doesn't happen until Chris is earning over a set amount.

In order to help students even further, some universities are giving back a proportion of their tuition fee income in the form of bursaries to help needy students, i.e. those who are eligible for the full maintenance grant.

However, since universities can set their own level of support in this way, it is important that you and Chris make early contact with universities that Chris is proposing to apply to in order to determine the exact level of support available.

There are yet other sources of funding. Some companies and the armed services may support students through university in return for a commitment to work for or serve with them in the future. For these, Chris will have to contact the intended firm or service directly.

Help may also be available if Chris is studying specific subjects, and universities should know about this. Examples are funding from the NHS for health-related courses, and from the Department for Children, Schools and Families for courses leading to Qualified Teacher Status. Educational trusts and charities might be able to help too, depending on Chris's course, university and financial status – contact the Educational Grants Advisory Service
(*www.egas-online.org.uk*) for specific advice.

Confused? Fees, bursaries, grants and loans – it's a fast moving field, a minefield even, and Chris will appreciate some help in finding her way through it. As we've said elsewhere … two heads are better than one.

Extra help …
In order to widen participation in under-represented groups among the undergraduate population, there are a number of other different types of support available for specific groups of students. Chris might be eligible for these.

If Chris is registered disabled consider the Disabled Students' Allowance and more details on this can be found at *www.direct.gov.uk/DisabledPeople*. The allowance covers a variety of additional expenses including extra costs associated with travel, the cost of a non-medical helper (for example someone to help with practical or studio work, or a note-taker) and special equipment or materials (for example tactile diagrams, computer software).

There is similar help for students who have either adult dependants or children – see Chapter 12 *Other sources of information*. These forms of assistance should be in place well before Chris starts her course. Encourage Chris to be proactive.

Access to Learning funds are generally available for students after they have already started their course. They are paid by the university and are targeted at students who have a low income and who need an extra income stream to allow them to finish their course. The specific conditions under which these grants can be given are outlined by the Department for Children, Schools and Families –
www.dfes.gov.uk/studentsupport/administrators/dsp_section_6.shtml
and the funds can be used to: meet specific course and living costs which are not already met from other

sources; help if students are in financial hardship; provide emergency payments for unexpected financial crises; and help students who may be considering giving up their course because of financial problems.

While these funds are available for both full-time and part-time students, certain deserving students will be given preference. Broadly, these are: students with children, particularly lone parents; mature students; students from low-income families; disabled students; students who have a history of being in care; students who are homeless; and students in the final year of their course.

The support may be in the form of a non-repayable grant or a loan that has to be repaid, usually in the short term. If Chris has already started her course and is feeling the financial pinch, check whether she is eligible for this extra support. Remember, you'll get nothing if you don't ask!

... and is it really all worth it?

When we went to university the Government paid our fees *and* gave us a reasonably generous maintenance grant. A hike in income tax would be necessary for a similar system to operate now, given that many more people go to university. We don't remember many of our contemporaries, even those who had joined university to study 'vocational' subjects such as Architecture, Engineering, and so forth, arguing that the reason why they had come to university was to get a 'good' job.

Perhaps that was because in those days graduate jobs were relatively available and the competition far less intense than it is today. A recent Psychology graduate of our acquaintance applied for a temporary position in clinical psychology – he was one of over 600 applicants. Another post that was part-time with just two days a week attracted nearly 200 applicants.

Nowadays job prospects are just as important to the university applicant as the subject of the course itself. Staffing stands at careers' fairs is now a real 'eye-opener' for us. Questions from potential students focus on graduate employment rates, the range of openings available, starting salaries and pension provision, rather than on details of the courses and the individual modules.

So why should Chris go to university? Is there a financial edge? It is often argued that a graduate will earn more in his/her lifetime than a non-graduate with A levels. Even as recently as 2007 the maximum differential was thought to be about £340,000, for Medicine and Dentistry. The average was about £160,000, but it has also been acknowledged that for some subject areas, particularly in the arts, the difference could be as little as £35,000. At those sorts of differential it is worth asking the question, "Is it really worth the hassle?" It is possible that as the UK moves towards 50% of school-leavers entering university, this differential will diminish and therefore one of the main reasons why school-leavers go to university – to obtain a higher salary and earn more over their lifetimes – will be lost. But the crystal ball gazers also tell us that the demand for highly trained individuals will increase and so the differential may even increase!

Another aspect to consider is that many jobs require a degree, any degree, just to get on the shortlist: there are now many jobs that are *only* open to graduates.

The outgoings are also difficult to estimate, as you'll know if you've attempted to help Chris with her budget. Top-up fees plus accommodation, travel, books, broadband, day-to-day living expenses, etc. make it almost impossible to calculate an exact figure.

A best guess is that students who started university courses in September 2006 are likely to face bills of about £35,000 for a three-year course. Personal experience suggests that this is about right.

So if you really want to do the sums, go ahead. But you won't know Chris's lifetime increase in earnings and you can only 'best guess' at the cost of university education.

Nevertheless, our back-of-an-envelope sums above suggest that for most students, going to university will be financially beneficial. But remember that plumbers currently command high salaries and you do not need a degree to be a plumber… yet.

Debt

Part-time jobs are a good way to stave off student debt, but even so, the average debt on graduation is currently thought to be about £15,000 – owed to the Student Loan Company, credit card companies and, through generous overdraft facilities, to high street banks. Unfortunately both these last two sources of money require that the student pays off the debt shortly after graduation or face high interest charges.

Adding to the debt woes of the recent graduate are then the complications of the four Ps, property, pensions, partners and parenthood. Most graduates would aspire to own their own property shortly after graduation, having spent the last three years in perhaps cramped conditions, sometimes primitive and usually with shared facilities. But a house of Chris's own requires both a deposit and comparatively high mortgage repayments.

Pensions are another peak on the financial horizon and though young graduates – and old lags like us – are loath to consider them, they do have to be faced very soon after graduation.

You will know when Chris has finally grown up when you receive a phone call that starts off, "Mum … what do you know about pensions?" Be prepared! Get some advice! There is now lots of good financial advice on pension planning for young adults, and it's well worth anticipating the phone call that will surely come. The partners and parenthood we leave to you!

Alternatives to university

Chris could leave school at 16 or 18 and join the job market with non-university qualifications. She would certainly be starting on the bottom rung of any career ladder but in three to five years (the time it might take her to progress through a university degree) she could expect to have progressed a significant way.

She would have joined what is euphemistically called the 'University of Life'. There are enough examples of people who have made it to the top, particularly in the business field, that this is a route that should not be dismissed lightly. Prime examples are Sir Richard Branson, reputedly worth £3 billion and Sir Philip Green, the chief of British Home Stores, reputedly worth £4.9 billion.

These 'entrepreneurial spirits' have not only made it to the top, but have also made a fortune along the way. In an interview Sir Philip Green referred to a "degree in common sense" as being an important asset for employees – the implication being that a university degree certificate may be worth less than the common sense and experience that the workplace gives its employees.

We're not trying to put you off sending Chris to university; we're merely trying to open your eyes.

CASE STUDY – JAMIE
Jamie was a very outgoing Drama student who seemed to have a wide circle of friends. At the start of his first year he settled in well and seemed to be a good prospect for academic success.

Assignments came in on time and were of a high standard, frequently word-processed when most of his colleagues were content to produce hand-written work.

First year examinations at the end of semester one in January didn't go so well, however, and he failed one exam and did rather poorly in another – nowhere near as well as the performance in his coursework would have indicated. Then, as semester two progressed, his coursework started to fall apart. Gone was the precision of the first semester and he started to miss deadlines.

Attendance was also poor and he seemed uninterested in theatre work and seminars – in stark contrast to his performance in the first semester. It was noticeable that he seemed to distance himself from other students, leaving lectures separately from the main group, for example.

A tutorial half-way through semester two was organised over a leisurely cup of coffee and the conversation started to drift to non-academic matters.

A few of Jamie's friends outlined their part-time jobs, mainly in fast-food joints or supermarkets and mainly for about 10-12 hours per week, usually at weekends. But Jamie remained very quiet and it was only after the other students had left that he admitted to the tutor that he was in severe financial difficulties caused by his on-line gambling habit.

Although he had a full student loan and grant, access to on-line gambling sites through the university computer suites had been his downfall and the money had rapidly evaporated. To make ends meet he had got a job – full-time! He was working a basic 35 hours a week plus occasional overtime. Given that a student is expected to do about 40 hours of academic work this meant that he should have been working about 75 hours a week.

While he had originally planned his financial commitments well for the year, he could not have foreseen the rapidity with which his addiction developed.

When jobs start to interfere with academic progress we have to take notice and luckily Jamie was open to support. The fact that he was prepared to admit that he had an addiction was important. Student Services quickly put him in touch with Gamblers Anonymous but, like any addiction, there are no quick fixes. They also arranged for him to talk to one of their financial support officers who was able to help Jamie to reorganise his debts and thus enable him to reduce the hours he worked to a more manageable 18 hours a week.

A frank discussion with his bank manager was essential and went well – his overdraft facilities were extended. In the short term he was also helped by the student hardship fund, though this was in the form of vouchers so that he wouldn't be tempted to use the money to feed his addiction.

Moving to a less attractive part of the city that was both closer to the university and to his place of work meant that he could save money on rent and also he could sell his car.

To recover from such a set-back is a long haul and it was not until the start of his final year, nearly 18 months after the first alarm bells started to ring, that he was on a reasonably stable financial footing and his work had returned to the promise shown in the first semester of his first year. Interestingly, on graduation Jamie decided to join a national charity in a fund-raising/administrative role. This was not particularly well-paid but he chose to take the job because his experiences had highlighted just how important support is for people in difficulties and facing stress, and he wanted to 'give something back'.

Students coming forward with financial difficulties to academic staff are comparatively rare. Most students' problems relate to teaching, learning and assessment issues, illness or personal problems. Sometimes, however, financial difficulties start to influence academic performance and that's when we become alerted that something is wrong.

While the outcome for Jamie was successful – perhaps in a way he'd never have guessed – it could all have been disastrous. It's difficult for anyone to admit that they have an addiction, but early disclosure would have helped Jamie greatly.

While Chris might not want to disclose a financial difficulty to you, after all it might be your money that has been 'lost', she should be aware that campus professionals can and do help. Be prepared, through budgeting, and know where the professional help is.

What advice should you give?

There is no doubt that there is still an earnings advantage in having a degree, even though that advantage may be diminishing. Additionally, a degree opens up avenues and career pathways that would remain closed to the non-graduate.

It's also easier to switch pathways ... a degree is evidence of an enquiring mind, a mind that is not closed to new ideas and new ways of doing things. Of course, some career pathways demand a degree, such as teaching and medicine and here there are no alternatives.

One other advantage of a university course is that it gives Chris the opportunity to experience a learning culture that hopefully will stay with her throughout her life … 'life-long learning'. She will also make life-long friends and have a good social life without the attendant stresses of later life – kids, a mortgage, job-security, etc. It's very difficult to put a price on that kind of experience.

Even at £35,000, a university education still represents excellent value for money. If Chris is wavering about getting a university degree or going straight into a job then our advice would still be to argue for the former.

Take the time to assimilate the complex information available and, if necessary, take advice from those in the financial field – bank managers, citizens' advice bureaux, etc. Then, if Chris is undecided, a thorough analysis of pros and cons would seem to be the way forward.

But can the benefits of a university education be measured in pounds anyway? That's for you and Chris to decide!

Chapter 10

Avoiding and recovering from a poor start

Every year in the UK, somewhere between 7% and 11% of students leave Higher Education within one year of joining. The public perception of this figure is often that it is unacceptably high. Compared with other countries, however, it is relatively low. In part this is because the UK still has a selection system prior to entry – many other countries don't.

This means that, ideally, all of those who enter Higher Education in the UK should be academically able to complete a course of study – they have been selected on this basis. The exception is the non-selective Open University. By and large the selection works: most students who drop out of university don't fail on academic grounds. But universities don't select students on their abilities to survive in a university environment.

In Chapter 1 *Introduction – what this book is about* we said that more people go to university now than ever before. This expansion has been at some cost and one of these costs is that a greater proportion of those who now enter university are not well-suited to the courses and/or careers that they have mapped out for themselves (or, perhaps more crucially, have *not* mapped out for themselves).

Some of these students decide to leave and some fail at the end of year one. This Chapter is about helping you to guide Chris so she can avoid a poor start, and about how you can help if she does make a poor start.

So how can Chris avoid a poor start? To answer that you need to understand *when* the poor start happened. Yes, that's right *"happened"* not *"will happen"*, because the seeds of success and failure will have been sown many years ago. Although it will never be too late for Chris to succeed, she may find it difficult because of the way in which she has been prepared for Higher Education, by her school, and by her family – not just you but the extended family – and friends. These will have moulded her attitudes towards work and study, towards what she is prepared to do to achieve her ambitions and towards what activities she finds enjoyable.

Throughout this book we've been stressing what you and Chris need to do to ensure her success. Much of that applies here, but repeating that information would be a waste of your time, so instead we've noted some *additional* items to consider.

A less than ideally supportive environment

Chris may have already had a poor start. Students with good qualifications on entry are more likely to graduate. That may not surprise you. It has also been shown, however, that poor entrance qualifications are closely associated with coming from families from the lower socio-economic groups and coming from low participation neighbourhoods.

It may seem unfair but students who come from relatively poorer backgrounds achieve less at school and subsequently tend to drop out or perform poorly at university. Think about this. We're definitely not saying that students from poorer backgrounds lack ability.

The 'middle classes' in the UK 'send' about 80% of their offspring to university. Are middle-class kids inherently brighter? No, of course not – it's about the environment they have been exposed to and what is 'normal' to them in educational and aspirational terms.

It can be argued of course that poorer neighbourhoods do not attract the best teachers and that families with no history of Higher Education are less able to prepare the next generation for the experience of university. It is difficult to tell your offspring what to expect and how to behave if you have not been there and not done that.

Moving anyone from a familiar environment to a strange one can have two effects.

The first is stimulating. Change and challenge, of themselves, are exciting; they can encourage people to achieve extraordinary feats. If the change is too much, however, then a second effect can be bewilderment and demotivation – an inability to cope.

How much is too much varies from person to person and the extent of change depends both on the environment from which the student comes and that to which the student is going. It is best to prepare yourself therefore, for the fact that the more unfamiliar Chris is with universities and study in Higher Education the less likely she is to graduate. This, of course, is where our advice might be key.

Part of the solution to culture shock, and that is what it is, is familiarity and this can be addressed long before Chris goes to the university. Visit university campuses. They are all open. Go to your local university. Have a wander round. When there are open days, encourage Chris to go, even if she is not thinking of attending that particular university.

Encourage her to learn what campus life is like from anyone and anything you can – your colleagues, former school friends, blogs, etc.

We do not really understand, as parents, how much influence we have over our kids. A few of your off-hand remarks about graduate unemployment or the value of a degree in Golf Course Management may well colour your kids' attitudes to the value of a higher education more than you might think. Also, what are their friends saying to them?

We know of small groups of able children that didn't try for university because that was 'uncool'. You and Chris's friends not only affect how willing she is to go on to Higher Education but also the commitment to it that she develops once she is there. Chris needs to expect to have a valuable experience and she can get that expectation from you.

So be careful. Careless talk costs marks; worse it could cost a career, one you never knew might be possible! You need to develop a sustained interest in, and enthusiasm for, the benefits of the opportunities offered by a higher education. Use this book to help you!

Leaving early?

When students wish to leave they will often talk it over with academic staff. Many want to leave for understandable reasons and it is often the best thing for them to do.

Here are the three main things that they tell us and how you could go about helping to solve the problem before it arises.

"I'M ON THE WRONG COURSE"

In the first few weeks of the first term this is probably the most common complaint. Disillusionment is a common cause. Students often do not understand what a particular subject will be like.

They know what Forensic Science is only because they have watched fictional accounts on the television. What they may not know is that it requires a fundamental understanding of chemistry and physics which they will have to study in some depth before they get to the more interesting things. Computing Science is not about writing computer games. It is about logic, language structures and databases.

Some students find out what a career in their chosen subject is really going to be like only during their first industrial placement. They have not previously understood that, for example, nurses really do have to work unsocial hours, that patients do die, and that some of their colleagues may be disillusioned too. And that ambition to work in a laboratory that seemed so glamorous and interesting at the careers talk might merely consist of pouring water into a machine and printing off the results to give them to someone else to interpret.

Avoiding the shock of realising that the course or workplace doesn't meet Chris's expectations is not that difficult. It is about researching the course and, where appropriate, the profession. Students who have done their homework to find out what the course entails and have visited workplaces are much less likely to have these problems.

The value of short-term work experience offered by some schools is invaluable here and such experience should be chosen with care to help Chris make more informed choices later on. No student who has researched courses thoroughly should be disillusioned.

"I DON'T LIKE IT HERE"

Living away from home for the first time can be unexpectedly difficult for some; having to work and reside with a group of total strangers from different backgrounds and expectations can be disorienting for others. Leaving friends, relations and relationships behind can engender hidden stresses no matter how well-prepared students think they might be.

Again the solution lies in the preparation. There is very little a university can do for those students who are living away from home but who are not prepared to *leave* home.

There are, however, counselling services that can help individuals come to a more realistic view of their circumstances, especially the time scale involved. Three years is not very long, although when you're young and standing on the threshold of it, it may seem to stretch forward for ever.

Conversely, students living at home may feel themselves excluded from university life. Their colleagues in class may be chatting about their previous evening's exploits at society events, or more probably at the local pubs or clubs, whereas home-dwellers are still living the same lives they had at school. Although the finance will always be an issue, just because a student goes to a university in their hometown does not mean that they have to live at home.

The solution to these problems is as obvious as it can be difficult. Students need to join in and the initiative lies with them. Even something as simple as being a class representative can help apparent outsiders integrate.

So if Chris suggests that she does not really feel part of her class then suggest she volunteers for such a position – there are often vacancies. Most universities now offer formal training for the role which she can add to her CV. Everybody gains!

"I DIDN'T KNOW WHAT TO EXPECT"

This is the refrain from students who fail, especially in year one. Academic failure is not a disaster; it is a warning. As we saw in Chapter 6 *Assessment*, university assessments are not designed so that a proportion of students will fail them.

Our expectation is that all will pass. Students who fail often say that they did not understand what was expected of them or did not appreciate the standard of work required.

Unfortunately our communication with students is often very passive, i.e. we make information *available* for students. We give course notes on web pages or on handouts, or we give feedback on assessments in footnotes, or even on notice boards. We expect students to seek out the information; it would be rare for university staff to check that individual students have read and understood this information – it's about maturity again.

So the advice is that if Chris expresses any doubts about anything or asks your advice about the standard of work required, she needs to go and ask a member of academic staff, preferably the one most closely associated with the work.

Discussing issues with fellow students is also a good idea but we sometimes find that "circles of incompetence" develop. These occur when groups of students form independent learning communities and unfortunately learn the wrong thing! Small student learning communities are excellent in supporting learning but they need to be grounded in good information. Chris should ask and discuss!

Academic failure

Sounds dreadful, doesn't it? All that work and nothing to show for it. Imagine how much Chris will dread that phone call home, or walking in through the door to announce that she has failed. What can you do; what can you say? The first thing to do is not to panic and to analyse what exactly has happened. Get her to write it down.

What has she passed and what has she failed? She will be unlikely to have failed all her assessments. And there will be many ways in which she can turn this around. Let's consider both failure in coursework and after the examinations, i.e. at the end of the academic year.

Failure in coursework

Re-visit what we said in Chapter 6 *Assessment*. Can you spot weaknesses in her work using the 'feed-forward' Chris was supplied with? Has she discussed her failings with those who assessed her work?

We all commonly learn by trial and error. We expect students to make mistakes but we expect them to learn from them as well. Poor coursework is not a disaster. It is actually an opportunity for learning. If Chris does poorly in her coursework then she needs to analyse what is going wrong as early as possible. What follows is what some students have told us.

"IT WASN'T WORTH DOING"

In year one she will probably get a series of tasks to perform very early on in the course. This is so we can monitor how she is doing. These pieces of work may be for trivial numbers of marks and some students fail merely because they do not hand them in.

Why waste time on it when it is only worth 5%? The answer to this might be that what she would have learned from this 5% piece of work might have been crucial in completing the 25% piece later in the term. Most students who fail coursework fail not because their coursework is poor, but because they never hand it in at all.

"I DIDN'T KNOW WHAT TO DO"

University staff are human; worse – many are young and inexperienced, and even worse than that, they may be untrained as teachers. Sometimes they are not very good at telling students *exactly* what they want them to do.

If Chris has found, through failure in coursework, that she didn't understand what was expected, she should persist in finding out. Ask and discuss! Academic staff will not be unsympathetic.

In reviewing assessed work it should be clear from the feedback whether it was the mechanics of the task itself which caused the problems or the understanding of the subject.

Are there words like *"inaccurate"*, *"wrong"* or *"it is not as simple as this"* on the work indicating that Chris just got it wrong. Or is it peppered with words like *"irrelevant"*, *"answer the question"*, *"you should have discussed…"* or *"this should be in essay format"* which means that the task itself was misunderstood. A deficit of writing skills is often indicated by phrases like *"I don't understand this"*, *"ambiguous"*, *"poorly structured"*, *"inadequate reference list"* or *"try reading this out loud"*.

Coursework, however, is not always written. Many of us now use group work. When students eventually get a job they will not be sitting at desks writing academic essays or answering multiple-choice questions. They will largely be working with colleagues to solve problems. So some assessment will be based on the contributions students make to joint outcomes.

Students may be asked to assess the contribution made by their colleagues in the group. Mostly the marks are equally shared but occasionally a student does not join in or does not pull his or her weight and can lose marks. See *CASE STUDY – MOHAMMED* in Chapter 7 *Teaching*. You might need to encourage Chris to reflect on what she could have done differently to perform such tasks better, and this may be to do with co-operating with other students as much as with the traditional academic skills.

She should not worry about inequalities in workloads between students in a group. Life's like that. Those who contribute the most, learn the most and it will pay off in the end, either in a better performance in the assessment or in terms of Chris's personal development.

So, poor or failing work is not all the same. It might demonstrate a lack of knowledge and understanding, the task itself may have been misinterpreted, or the student may lack the necessary communication or team working skills. But failure can be used to highlight modes of work with which Chris is uncomfortable.

Once Chris understands the problem then the solution is easier to arrive at. You can help here. You may not have a good grasp of the subject material but the chances are that you have read much more than Chris, have a wider vocabulary, and have spent years working with other people.

You can help merely by asking her questions. What does this mean? Are these things actually linked? Does the work have a beginning, middle and an end; does a paragraph address a single idea; how was this assessed; who did you work with, what did they do? You will have more experience of all these things than Chris merely by virtue of having lived longer. Use your experience.

Failure at the end of the year

Most universities will have examinations at the end of each year in May or June. Some will have half of the examinations in January or February. The examination marks are combined with coursework marks to produce an overall score for each module, though Chris will probably know how well she has done in her coursework well before the examinations. What can you do if Chris fails?

First, you might want to help Chris to appeal if you or she thinks an injustice has been done. You'll need a copy of the university's regulations on assessment – Chris should have been given this information – and you'll need to find out what the appeals procedure is.

Normally Chris will have to be quick. Appeals are normally heard within a week or two of the examination results being known and they normally depend on evidence that was not available to the examining board when the original decision was made.

If there were extenuating circumstances (such as an illness or injury to Chris or a close relative, death of a close relative, trauma such as being mugged, extreme weather preventing travel, or some domestic upheaval such as burglary) related to Chris's performance in the assessment then these should have been made known to the university before the results were published.

Universities do not look favourably on students who decide that there were extenuating circumstances only *after* they know they have failed something. Anecdotes abound in university common rooms of the student whose grandparents regularly die on the eve of examinations, of the cluster of students all of whom appear to have the same uncle with the same illness and of cars that suddenly develop faults on the way in to examinations.

Do not encourage Chris to appeal just because there is an appeals process. Make sure there is a reasonable excuse first. Oh, and usually computer malfunction doesn't count either ... encourage Chris to keep back-up copies of everything, perhaps by e-mailing things to herself.

The university will notify Chris (make sure the address the university holds for her is up to date) of its decision on her progress. The most common one is that she has passed and can proceed to the next level of study. But there are others ... ...

"RE-SIT AN EXAMINATION OR RESUBMIT COURSEWORK"

The exam board will have reviewed Chris's work and decided where the deficiencies lie. The board will indicate what she needs to do now to show that she can do *all* those things (the learning outcomes) the module descriptions specify. Remember what we said in Chapter 6 *Assessment* about how our courses are described: we specify the minimum requirements. And failure means that the minimum has not been achieved.

Re-sitting represents an opportunity to show that this minimum standard can be reached. Chris shouldn't expect exactly the same exam or essay title, etc., as before, but the assessment should test the same abilities.

Don't forget that students re-sit to pass only: they will only gain the minimum number of marks required to expunge a failure, usually 40%. It does not matter how brilliantly a re-sit is completed; only a mark of 40% will be entered. This is to avoid the situation where students who initially fail can do better than those who pass at the first attempt.

"REPEAT THE YEAR"

This might involve all modules or only those Chris has failed. Repeating the year can be with attendance or without. "With attendance" means that she will have to start the year all over again and complete all the assessments for all the modules she is taking again.

This can be a demoralising experience and she will need strong support from friends and family. Her classmates will all (or mostly) have moved on a year and she will be left to re-establish social contacts with a new class. It delays her entry into the workplace and may have other financial consequences. If she is recommended to repeat "without attendance" then she should discuss with academic staff precisely what she is being asked to do because she may be free to get a job for the year and the financial consequences will not be as great as those incurred by having to attend.

Many students who are recommended to repeat a year, especially if it is the first year, will choose to re-think their options and re-apply for other courses in other universities depending on their own diagnosis of what their problems might be. It may be during this process that Chris would need someone sympathetic to discuss things with.

"Change course"

The board of examiners may take the view that Chris is a worthy student but is on the wrong course. A way forward may even be worked out for her. If she has failed to pass a year, however, it is likely that she will have to start from scratch on a new course, though she may be able to use the credit gained from those modules she has passed.

Sometimes lower level courses are recommended. For instance, if a student struggles with a degree course then an HND (Higher National Diploma) or Foundation degree may be recommended. These represent real opportunities for students to stay in Higher Education and to benefit from the vocational experiences that these qualifications carry.

Talk the options over with Chris. If she's not suited to university level study, think seriously about other paths. What's best for her, *not* what's best for you?

"Withdraw from university"

This is an extremely rare decision and is only likely following no improvement subsequent to the other decisions. But still all is not lost. If she has passed sufficient elements of her course she might be awarded a Certificate or Diploma of Higher Education, which she could 'cash in' for study towards an Honours degree at another university.

Even with no formal qualification to show from her time at university, if Chris is determined (and has the finances) the door will open eventually. She could take a break and return to Higher Education later in life, or try immediately for a fresh start at another university.

CASE STUDY – NICK

Nick did not make friends easily and he preferred to rely on his own resources and work by himself. He had done well at A levels and this was all down to his own hard work – and he knew it! He went to university to study Marine Science and worked strategically. By that we mean that he found out what he needed to do and just did that: a bare minimum.

The two Chemistry modules were no problem. He understood the chemistry because he had done most of it before at A level. The Statistics course was manageable. It was relatively simple and mainly involved learning what to do and when. Other modules were simply an extension of the biology syllabus he had already studied at A level.

Attendance earned no marks, so he did not attend and although the staff chased him a little, they were friendly enough and merely expressed curiosity about any problems he was having.

He did not tell them that the real problem was that he had decided to carry on with his part-time job so he could earn some money to keep his car on the road. In any case, most of his lecturers put their notes on the internet and he could download them at home.

He believed he could learn enough to pass the examinations and the coursework would look after itself.

It was the Skills module that let him down. The tutorials were on a Friday afternoon and he managed to get to one or two by swapping shifts with colleagues at work. Part of the assessment was the preparation of a poster, a common form of communication in the scientific community. The details are presented on a display board and the audience reads the poster and then the presenters of the poster are available to answer questions about it.

The poster was to be presented by a group and both the process of its production and the final product were assessed. The 'process' was assessed through the submission of brief minutes of the meetings held between the students to discuss the development of the poster.

The 'final product' (the poster) was self-assessed by the students who allocated each other marks; the marks were then reviewed by the tutor to ensure fair play. Nick missed the tutorial in which the groups were established and the elements of group work discussed, and was assigned to a group in his absence.

The other members of the group organised a meeting to discuss how to divide up the research necessary to gather in the information to put into the poster, but it was at a time when Nick could not attend.

The group continued to meet without him. When the tutor asked about progress within the groups he was told that Nick must have joined up with another group.

The tutor got a surprise when Nick submitted a short piece of written work as part of the poster assessment. It was quite well-written, but Nick's piece did not address the specific issues discussed in class or the assessment criteria. It was inevitable that his mark would not be high.

Nick was not there when the posters were assessed and the other members of his group did not assign him any marks – how could they? Also, since Nick didn't go to the meetings, he couldn't get marks for the minutes of those meetings either.

As a result of his poor engagement with the poster exercise he failed the coursework for the Skills module. There was no possibility of re-sitting the poster element since it was based on group work and he was the only one who had failed this element.

Unfortunately, the ability to work in groups was one of the learning outcomes of the module and he could not demonstrate that by working by himself. The board of examiners had little option but to ask him to repeat the year with attendance so he could show that he could indeed work with fellow students.

He started the first year again and changed his part-time job so that he could work more flexibly. In particular, he tried to attend most of the tutorial sessions. Old habits die hard however, and his attendance tended to drift off. After all, the notes were familiar and he thought he knew most of it. At least he was there when the groups were formed this year so he knew who else was in the group.

The staff kept a closer watch on his attendance. When the tutor discovered that Nick had not attended a group meeting he sought Nick out to warn him of the consequences of his continued behaviour. Nick started to attend the group meetings and, although working in the group did not suit him, he persisted and eventually passed the module.

We can learn three lessons from Nick's story. The first is that what may seem like a trivial problem can quickly build up into a big one if left. Nick was supposed to be a full-time student. It was assumed that he was available for tuition during normal working hours.

He made a series of bad decisions about his attendance and his ability to cope with the consequences. Non-attendance at most things can be dealt with. Notes can be supplied and reading recommended. University staff cannot, however, deal with non-participation. Non-participation feeds on itself. After a student has missed a few sessions, especially small group sessions, it is much harder for him to re-join because his presence will be noticed in a way that his absence was not.

The second lesson arises as a result of the uncomfortable feeling Nick had with some of the things he was being asked to do. He had not collaborated with colleagues before and found the prospect of relying on others and giving away what he had learned quite disturbing.

But this simply reflects real world work scenarios and it is thus appropriate to assess group work at university. Nick was unfortunate in that, on this occasion, it formed a critical part of the assessment. Nick should have been more aware of what was being asked of him, uncomfortable or not.

The third lesson is that many academic staff will assume that students can work independently from the start. Many students have come to university through a secondary education system in the UK that encourages dependency on teachers. Most new students are adaptable enough to cope with the change, but some are not. University work is supposed to be challenging right from the start.

There are ways of making it easier by telling students all they need to know, by limiting the assessment to areas that students find comfortable and by taking responsibility for organising all aspects of student learning. But if we do that, the students will remain teacher-dependent and be as institutionalised when they leave university as when they entered it.

When students run into problems, however, there are things that staff can do to support them, perhaps by paying closer attention. But this support cannot continue since it runs counter to the graduate qualities we are attempting to develop. These support systems must always be seen, therefore, as short term. Nick's independence in having a job and a car should have applied to his studies too – he got the balance wrong.

And finally …

A poor start, then, can result from a lack of commitment, a lack of understanding about the nature of the work involved or, more rarely, a lack of ability. All these will require a serious review of what Chris wants to get out of university. If she is not prepared to commit her time and energy to the course or the university then perhaps she has made some poor decisions and needs to re-think them.

If she has done poorly merely because she did not understand what was being asked of her then now is the time to resolve to ask questions until things become clear. Finally, if Chris really cannot understand the subject material then a lower level course or a different subject area might be called for.

We have assumed that some sort of failure will trigger these thoughts. Even if she passes everything but not as well as she expected or is discontented, the end of year one might be a time to review her earlier decisions to see if they were indeed the right ones. Is she happy with the course, does it hold out the vocational prospects she expected, will she cope with the topics that will be introduced in year two, is she happy with the lifestyle that she has adopted? Could things be changed?

One of our sons changed from Chemistry to Computer Science after year one, not because he failed anything, but because he found he had the aptitude and that the practical end of computing fitted in better with his work pattern.

No matter how well Chris is doing, 'taking stock' is always worthwhile. It is often only by studying a subject in depth that its true nature is revealed. Students often become fascinated with their chosen subject and this drives them to excel. But by the same token students can realise that they have made a serious error of choice. But life is full of mistakes and you should support Chris if she changes her mind about her chosen course of study.

Darwin, Einstein and more than one President of the UK's premier scientific body, The Royal Society, have changed their minds about their courses of study. It is, therefore, important to check early on whether Chris is satisfied with her choice. If she isn't, then the best advice to her, and to you, is not to panic, but to seek advice from as many parties as you, and especially she, can – but quickly – because the longer the delay, the fewer options she will have.

Ask and discuss! This situation is not uncommon and it is very rare for such a student to withdraw from university. Admittedly, the best case scenario – in terms of unproductive time – involves Chris realising after the first lecture that the course is not for her. Many students find themselves in this position and a few days later are enrolled on a related, or even wholly unrelated, course.

Often the realisation comes after the first few assessments, but even if the light dawns after much of the first year has elapsed, all is not lost. Chris should re-think what course might be for her. Re-investigate the prospectus. Take soundings. Ask and discuss! Swapping to another course is probably easier than you think or she thinks. Chris should talk to whoever runs the courses she might be interested in swapping to. Universities are usually keen to retain students who have enrolled with them, even if this means switching to a totally different subject.

It is not unheard of for students of science to switch to humanities courses, and vice versa, but swapping to a similar course, e.g. within the humanities, or within the sciences, is more common.

The closer the two academic courses are and the earlier Chris wants to swap, the smoother the transition. But if she does find herself on the wrong course, the mature thing to do is to admit this and to start to seek solutions, even if the realisation came late. Ask and discuss!

Lastly, be assured that no matter how poor a start Chris might have, all is never lost. There is always another route through the system – other universities are available and study at one may 'count' towards a degree at another. Students who persist in asking questions rarely fail. If she is committed enough she will succeed.

Chapter 11

What next?

It's late September. Chris has been in her room for the last two days "packin'". Enrolment for Chris's final year is in a week and it's now time to get things together. It's been a long haul: two years for GCSEs, two years for her entry qualifications, and now the early years of her degree successfully completed ... just one more year to go and then it will all be over. But what happens next? Where does Chris go from here? Is it out of your hands? What is the next critical event and the next transition boundary to overcome?

Once again it will be easier for Chris than for you. She has the enthusiasm of youth on her side ... "everything will be fine, stop worrying" ... but you know better or think you know better. Luckily for Chris, youthful enthusiasm isn't all that's available and this chapter explores how universities support students in preparing for the 'world of work' and finding a suitable position after leaving university.

We will be examining the major options that are available to graduates and, of utmost importance, what you can do to help Chris through a difficult decision-making time. After all, in 2006, for example, approximately 260,000 new graduates joined the job market, and you may want to give Chris a little bit of an advantage.

Imagine that Chris's degree programme is complete. She's graduated. So what's next for her? Is that the time to be thinking about a career? Emphatically 'No!': a terrible approach, doomed to failure. To secure a 'what's next?', you and Chris need to be considering the future and the 'now' now!

The careers service

Careers services in universities are now regarded as a professional service. We make this point because the change in recent years has been substantial. Chances are that when you were at school the careers service was pretty poor. When one of us said he wanted to go to university, the careers teacher said, "there's no harm in aiming high."

Another of us fancied being a vet, but was told by his careers teacher of the impossibility of such a career in the industrialised West Midlands and that he should perhaps be a bank teller. At university, it really wasn't much better. He had a talk at the start of the final year that more or less said that any jobs notified to the Careers Service would be posted on the 'Positions Open' notice board in one of the corridors. That was the sum total of his careers advice!

But can Chris expect much better? Skilled careers staff now offer advice, certainly in the later stages of school or college education. Similarly, at university professional careers staff provide up-to-date, relevant and timely information for undergraduates. The advice is tailored for the individual, so there's little point in us generalising here.

Although the careers services are good – we can't think of even one example of poor service – universities are varyingly good in the way they alert their students to the careers service. You can do the alerting if the university doesn't. Again the service is there for Chris. It is up to her to get the best from it.

CV building for beginners

Where universities structure their careers advice, students may be required to produce a Curriculum Vitae (literally their 'life race-track') – a statement of who they are, what their qualifications and achievements are, what their experiences are, and what skills they possess. If the university doesn't provide the structure, you can – encourage Chris to create a CV!

When compiling their CVs, students dutifully record their part-time work experience, if any. Jobs are listed in CVs with the dates, job titles and a short resumé of the tasks involved. But what students often miss out is the important range of job and life skills that they are acquiring along the way. And these can be very impressive indeed. Chris should be putting these skills in her CV. Life skills are acquired through virtually any form of employment, be it being part of a 'divoting' team – replacing divots on golf courses starting at five o'clock in the morning – or doing an overnight shift at an all-night garage.

Both these jobs require time management and team working skills and employers are looking for evidence that these have been honed. Is there scope for including Chris's organisational capabilities, for example, in prioritising her work and/or the work of others? Does she have responsibilities, for example, as a key-holder or in cashing-up, or for the training of others? We're sure you can think of other life skills to include.

Don't worry if Chris doesn't have a job; think about the life skills she has acquired through her programme of study. What is important is that Chris realises that the skills she is acquiring and has acquired, through study or perhaps part-time work, can look very impressive if described correctly in a CV. Try to tease these out of her if she isn't yet tuned in to the process. In the jargon, this is 'CV building', that is, identifying skills in both professional and personal life that can be included in a CV, at appropriate places, to enhance the CV by providing supporting evidence for the claims made.

It's not just the part-time job and study that yield suitable material. Is Chris a leader with a local youth group? Does she play sports to a reasonable level? Has she coached young children in her sport? Can she play a musical instrument? Has she learned a foreign language just for the fun of it? Has she taken part in helping un-housed people find sheltered accommodation? Or climbed Annapura? Or whatever.

Try to imagine yourself and Chris as recruiters for an organisation she might like to work for, or study at. What's going to impress you in a CV? And faced with many CVs that are superficially the same, what's going to make Chris's stand out? It could be that an awareness of the skills she possesses and an ability to rationalise them will be the key. It certainly won't be the fancy font or the coloured paper!

Progress files

The UK government of the 1990s was concerned about Higher Education and set up a commission to examine the state of education in British universities. This became known as the 'Dearing Report' and it was published in 1997. One of the recommendations was that:

... institutions of higher education ... develop a Progress File. The File should consist of two elements:
- *a transcript recording student achievement ...;*
- *a means by which students can monitor, build and reflect upon their personal development.*

Reflection is an important word and in this context means reviewing performance or tasks and trying to highlight those strengths and weaknesses that have contributed to how successfully the tasks have been completed. Reflection, if performed well, should allow the development of strategies to improve weaknesses and enhance strengths. It should be an important life skill to maintain and improve performance.

The Progress File (sometimes called Personal Development Planning) has been taken up in various guises in different universities, but the essence is that students should have an accurate and up-to-date account of their achievements and skills, as well as evidence that they have thought about their own development.

This becomes their Personal Development Plan (PDP). Central to this is the concept of CV building; it is here that students can start to provide the evidence of what they will be able to do and what they have already achieved.

Because the PDP is now so central to a student's career pathway it is introduced from year one and continued through to the final year (and, possibly, beyond into personal career development). In this way, CVs developed, or a skills audit completed, in year one are added to in successive years as more evidence or experience becomes available. Interestingly, while it is mandatory for universities to offer PDPs, the take-up by students is optional.

You can take an active role in Personal Development Planning by helping Chris to think about and record her thoughts on her work to date.

Experience tells us that students find this an incredibly difficult task and yet it is vitally important to improvement because if they do not realise what they have done and achieved, then they cannot plan how to improve.

Ask Chris about her PDP towards the end of her first year. And, most of all, help her think about her own performance. What went well? Why did it go well? What particular skills did Chris have that contributed to the success? Could there have been improvements? Why did it go badly? What could be done to improve things next time? Are there any skills that need to be developed for the future as a result of this poor performance? What strategy might be developed for ensuring that these skills are improved?

This represents 'quality time' with Chris and she will appreciate the efforts to help her. Remember, however, that the onus has to come from Chris. You should be there as a prompt – a 'facilitator' in the current educational jargon – rather than as a provider of solutions.

Career options and how to manage them

As Chris approaches her final year there are four basic options to consider.

1. For many students the most obvious option is to get a job immediately. This will be in your best interests – less worry, a firm financial footing – but will it be in Chris's? While there are jobs for graduates, particularly those with specialist degrees, a 'first degree' (Bachelor's degree, probably at Honours level) may not qualify Chris for a specific career, and without further qualifications she might find herself either re-training in employment or stuck in a dead-end, uninspiring job. It may be necessary, therefore, to consider further study.

2. Perhaps a further qualification (a 'second degree') is appropriate. These are broadly of two different types.

The first type is a specialist degree related to the first degree – Educational Psychology following a Psychology degree; Health Promotion following a Nutrition degree and so on. There are often two levels of these, post-graduate certificate/diploma and Master's courses. Both involve a taught element, with the Master's courses requiring an additional project element, usually investigating an original aspect of the subject.

Typically, the certificate and diploma courses are one academic year in length (September/October to

June) with Master's courses being a full calendar year (from September/October), or sometimes longer.

The second type is a conversion course. This is where the course is not related (or is only very loosely related) to the first degree and does not build on it – very popular conversion courses a few years ago were those in Information Technology (or Computing Science). These can also be taken at different levels, postgraduate certificate/diploma and Master's.

3. If Chris is awarded a degree at first or upper second class Honours level – or in exceptional cases at lower second class level – she may have the opportunity to undertake a period of research towards a doctorate (a Doctor of Philosophy – a PhD or a DPhil). These are usually of three years' duration, though average completion times are greater than this. In some fields the competition for places is very fierce and in others, not so. In any case, because of the very specialist nature of research, motivation and enthusiasm are key elements. To help prepare students for such an intense period of work, many universities now offer one-year Master of Research courses in which the specialist techniques applicable to a particular research area are acquired … thus the student approaches the research 'running'.

4. Of course, Chris may choose to take a gap year. We covered gap years in Chapter 2 *Student timeline: before university*, but that was focused on a gap before university. Increasingly, students are taking a year out after university in order to take stock of where they are at, where they wish to go, and to plan the most satisfying route to reach their goal. Who could blame them: for many they've had at least seven and up to nine years of hard work from the age of fourteen when GCSEs were started. Don't be disappointed if Chris takes this option. It may be better to ponder than to rush into something that her heart isn't really in. But make sure she uses the time wisely!

The final year is a busy time for students. Usually the majority of the marks for their degree (in some cases ALL the marks) will derive from work in their final year. An active social life is still important, but a finer balance now has to be struck.

Added to this is the problem of finding a job or obtaining a place for a further qualification and thus justifying all the work of the previous years at university. The general support that you have been providing over the last few years is still appropriate and important ... talk, talk, talk, discuss, discuss, discuss. Let's look at our four basic options in a little more detail and find out where you might help.

Finding a job

Encourage Chris to make use of the careers service. It can help in a number of ways including individual advice to students to help them to find their niche, perhaps including aptitude testing. It will also provide Chris with access to sources of job information; while many jobs are now listed on websites, a number of 'graduate-opportunity' publications are produced and many of the populist subject magazines have job listings as well. You could alert Chris to these too.

Most importantly, the careers service will offer advice on the application process itself ... form filling, CV preparation, letters of application, etc., and critically, advice on interviews (see next section).

Most universities are on the 'milk-round' (see *www.milkround.com*). This is where employers attend careers conventions and host recruitment stands at universities in the autumn and winter terms. Nearly all types of employer are represented at these fairs – large private companies, the public sector, many smaller organisations and, often, specialist firms recruiting particular graduates from particular universities.

While these often don't result in specific job applications, they are particularly important in opening students' eyes to the possibilities. Let's say Chris chose to do her first degree in Underwater Basket Weaving simply because it fascinated her at school and she wanted to learn more about it (incidentally, still a very good reason for going to university in the first place), but talking to some of the employers at a careers convention, she might find out that it is excellent training for the textile industry or marine exploration – options that she hadn't even considered.

Talking through options face-to-face with staff engaged in specific areas of industry is an excellent way of getting specialist careers advice. Ask Chris if she has seen any adverts for careers fairs/conventions and point out to her the advantages of attendance. Encourage her to go! And afterwards, why not talk through with her what she found out while things are still fresh in her mind?

Occasionally, the staff of a specific degree course will organise visits to the campus by specific employers to talk about careers. Often these organisations bring with them young graduates who have recently been taken on board. Again, opportunities like these should not be missed, as it is an excellent forum to discuss with recent graduates and human resource personnel the options available and how raw recruit graduates are treated in their first job.

Don't forget websites. Many employers now depend on websites to convey information about the services and opportunities they offer, rather than relying on printed materials that are difficult to effectively distribute and to keep up-dated. Internet search engines should locate specific companies or those within a specific industry and restricting the search geographically will help further.

Throughout this process there is a lot to discuss with Chris. What are the options? Has she found any suitable posts she could apply for? Does she want to stay in the same geographical area or is she prepared to move? Does she have an up-to-date CV? Offer to go through the CV with her, using the advice given above.

Offer to proof-read her letters and forms ... you may not be any better at grammar and punctuation than Chris but two heads are definitely better than one. Discussing these things with a sympathetic person will often be the best way to clarify things in Chris's mind. So even if you feel you have little of substance to contribute, you can still help by supporting Chris in her decisions.

Trying to get a job, as a new graduate (or as a student in the final year of a degree), is a time-consuming process. Chris should be prepared to fire off application after application and not worry too much about being 'picky'. If she is serious about getting a job then a low-paid one in an undesirable area might be the best way to get started on the career ladder. She can use this as a base to move up, using the experience to climb a rung or two. But it is important that she doesn't lose sight of the work that has to be completed for her degree and here you can help by talking through time-management issues with her.

Many final year students think that they cannot submit an application while they still have one pending – discourage that view! There is nothing wrong with putting in as many applications as you like but encourage Chris to be sensible and to stick with those where, if she were offered the job, she would be happy enough to accept it, even if it were only for a short time.

The interview

Since many universities no longer interview prospective students, a job interview may be Chris's first formal interview experience. Some careers services offer mock interviews. Encourage Chris to take up the option; it's a valuable learning experience. If you feel confident enough, conduct a mock interview with her yourself.

Remember that an interview, no matter how badly it goes, can be a very positive experience and much can be learned from it. From the careers service she will get advice on style of dress, what to take, how to handle particular questions and so on, but it is afterwards that you can be most useful. Put aside time to debrief Chris.

Try to encourage her, immediately after the interview, to list all the questions she was asked and to jot down her answers as best she can remember them. Get her to pay particular attention to questions where she felt she did badly *and* those that she confidently answered.

Go through these with her. Relate them to her strengths and weaknesses and identify areas for improvement for next time.

Which rather begs the question ... what are these interviewers looking for? As well as looking for competence in the subject – evidenced by the structure and content of the degree itself and how well Chris has performed in it – interviewers are looking for a wide range of other skills. Broadly, these are as follows:

1. Having the ability to work with limited supervision; to be independent.
2. Showing initiative and motivation.
3. Being able to solve problems.
4. Report writing, with succinct, clear, accurate and grammatically correct prose.

5.   Ability to give oral presentations and to communicate ideas and information clearly and unambiguously.

6.   Ability to work as part of a team and to take the lead when necessary.

7.   Maturity, with good social skills.

8.   Ability to make reasoned assumptions and interpret results effectively so that sound judgements can be made.

9.   Ability to accept criticism and praise in order to continuously improve through reflection.

These skills are what are often called 'graduate skills'. It's worth using these as a checklist so that when you go through Chris's CV or letters she has written, you can start to spot if these graduate qualities are to the fore.

Increasingly, employers are using testing to supplement interviews or are using testing to select candidates for interview. Such tests may be psychometric in nature or may test specific skills such as numeracy or verbal reasoning, or be very specialist and job related, for example data interpretation or manipulation.

Be prepared for these and get Chris to use the web, particularly blogs, to suss out exactly what the tests encompass. This isn't cheating – it's gaining an edge using publicly available information *and* it's being resourceful!

A second degree?

Second degrees are specialist degrees. If you thought Chris's first degree was specialised you might be surprised at just how specialised second degrees can be. Take stock. How does Chris see the future 'panning out' after this second degree? Will she be any further forward? Will the added expense be justified in terms of the range of options that will open up?

Ironically, a second degree may even restrict the possibilities.

These are important issues and make sure you talk them through. It will be another year, at least. A conversion course will often be a complete change of direction so it is important that the decision is taken in the light of all the evidence.

Without being too confrontational, talk this through too. Time for a list of Pros and Cons. We think that money here is less important than personal satisfaction, but bear in mind that, on average, a person with a second degree, including research degrees described in the next section, typically earns £70,000 - £80,000 more over a lifetime than a person with only a first degree.

In some cases, when Chris decides to study for a second specialist degree it may be the start of a very long period of training indeed. Take, for example, Clinical Psychology – a very important profession... and very stressful. The complete training period includes a first degree in Psychology. The graduate then has to gain, typically, a minimum of two years' work experience before undertaking a second specialist degree – a three-year National Health Service funded doctorate. Eight years in all, following entry to university. So think carefully about the timeline *after* university!

Going for research ...

Honours degree courses, by design, include some element of original investigation – research – either actual 'hands-on' or through the literature. For example, Jo had been studying for a degree in History and for her final-year dissertation she chose to look at the recently released government papers related to the start of the 'troubles' in Northern Ireland, particularly the role of the B specials.

She thoroughly enjoyed reading the documents and putting them together into a 'story', comparing the views of different opposing factions and evaluating decisions taken at the time in the light of subsequent events. Would she be capable of undertaking a research degree? Would she be able to cope with the stress?

While it might not seem stressful to be spending three years investigating an interesting topic, it can be. Much of the work is conducted independently, with little direct supervision.

The postgraduate may also be working in relative isolation compared with how life was as an undergraduate, where she would have been surrounded by fellow students following the same curriculum.

Jo decided to go ahead with the research degree and was lucky enough to get a grant. She is now in her first year of research but has discovered that what she found exciting as a final-year project, interspersed with other studies and activities, is rather tedious now that she is doing it full-time. And the staff expect her to be taking the initiative rather than guiding her all the time … and she wonders whether she has made the right choice. Does Chris know what she might be letting herself in for?

Like other second degrees, a doctorate may limit career options. For example, computer scientists work on very highly focused research topics and doctoral students in this area will be working on very specialist problems. At the end of their three-year research studentship, they might well be one of the world's experts in that topic but in the three (or four) years it has taken to gain the doctorate, the general area of computer science may have moved on significantly, or in a different direction, thus limiting job opportunities. Thus, doctorates in any subject need to be treated with care. They are extremely specialised and while many students will find employment with ease, others become so narrowly focused that finding a job that fits their talents can be difficult. Remember that a doctorate may allow Chris to learn a great deal about very little! The personal satisfaction may be immense but prospective employers may not be so impressed.

The doctorate isn't the only research degree available. Many choose to study for a Master's degree by research, an MPhil. These are similar in nature to a doctoral degree, but are at the slightly lower level of Masters and less is expected by way of originality.

Research Masters typically last one to two years and in some subjects may act as a springboard to a doctorate where, perhaps, the MPhil is not completed, but the study 'counts' towards the doctoral degree.

If Chris is interested in the research option, encourage her to talk to the staff that are supervising her final-year dissertation or research project; they will be the best to judge her suitability. If she is a very good student, the encouragement to do a research degree may actually come from the staff themselves, but it pays to discuss matters with them if there is no direct approach.

Remember, enthusiasm and motivation are the keys to a successful research student. You should be able to objectively judge these and advise Chris accordingly.

Taking a gap year – how you can help

And suppose Chris says she wants to 'clear her head' and take a year out. Don't look on this as a failure on Chris's part or a failure of the system. On the contrary, it suggests Chris is being very 'grown-up' about important life-forming decisions and is not prepared to take the most obvious route.

A gap year may also open up avenues that Chris might never have considered. Be prepared to be supportive and only be negative if Chris suggests putting herself in an area of potential danger. Then, as a parent, you probably have a right to sound negative.

On the other hand, at some time you do have to let go of the controls so that Chris can fly by herself: it's one of the hardest parts of having children, just like that day you waved her off at the start of her degree, three, four or even five years ago. How time flies, and believe us, it continues to gather speed!

CASE STUDY – KEVIN

Kevin was a working-class kid from an inner-city school and a nice guy. What he wasn't, we'll be honest, was a model student. Kevin wanted to be a doctor but his A level grades precluded that choice. Besides which, Kevin had very poor verbal communication skills and it would have been very difficult envisaging him in a patient-doctor relationship.

Wisely, Kevin entered 'clearing' to find a course in Biomedical Science and, with his half-decent grades including Chemistry A level, was accepted for a four-year Honours degree that included a compulsory placement year in a local hospital where he would be learning the 'tools of his trade'. But things did not go smoothly. Laziness and over-indulgence in the amber liquid meant that the first year was lost in an alcoholic fog.

Needless to say, he failed a number of his first-year modules. He was given the chance to – and did – repeat the outstanding coursework and his failed examinations at the end of the summer period, but didn't improve his situation substantially. He was still failing.

Biomedical Science supports the medical profession by providing analytical services to doctors and hospitals so that correct diagnoses can be made. Clearly, it is a service where you don't want poor students. So, the examination board took the view that while Kevin was capable of getting a degree, that degree could not be Biomedical Science.

They recommended he withdraw from the course, and advised that he could, if he so wished, transfer to another degree course.

Kevin then chose to study for a Biology degree, which had some teaching in common with Biomedical Science, particularly in the first year. Kevin thought he could coast through his new first year doing the minimal amount of work.

This was a big mistake and yes, you've guessed it, he found himself in exactly the same situation at the end of that year: failed modules. This time around Kevin did even worse in the re-sits and resubmissions of the coursework and the examination board had no alternative but to ask him to "repeat the first year with attendance".

So, two wasted years. What next? Kevin got through the first year this time, but then year two loomed. In Biology his third year was to be spent on placement. There were three options available: take an industrial placement, usually in the UK; take a foreign educational exchange within an EU country (Greece, The Netherlands, Ireland, Italy, Poland and Germany were on offer) or with the USA where he would attend a university or college and undertake relevant courses; or work in an approved research laboratory overseas.

One of the more prestigious approved research laboratories was on the west coast of America and Kevin decided to apply for one of their places. Kevin came through the telephone interview successfully and was offered a place in competition with students who appeared to be far better qualified both academically and in terms of skills development. The period abroad was fully funded by the host institution.

Luckily, Kevin came through the examinations and coursework associated with the second year modules without major mishap but his results still showed him to be a marginal third-class student. It is fair to say that the academic staff half expected Kevin to be returned from America within the month. But nothing untoward happened. He came home for Christmas and visited one of us, his placement tutor, and was unrecognisable.

Physically he had changed little, but he was now self-assured, confident, conscientious, enthusiastic, motivated and even ambitious. We spent a pleasant two hours talking about his work, his knowledge of the field, and what he was trying to do with a series of laboratory experiments. He was exceptionally impressive.

What had happened to bring about this massive transformation? Like nearly all students who undertake a year's work placement he had seen how his subject could be applied to real workplace situations … he had been 'turned on' by the subject. He had left failure behind and was starting completely from scratch and it changed him for ever.

To cut a very long story short, Kevin successfully completed his placement year – his mark for the 'logbook' element was the highest mark ever obtained by a student on his degree course. His end-of-placement seminar was a tour-de-force. He was able to talk about his work and his experience in a mature, interesting and authoritative manner and again it received the highest mark among his cohort.

He went into his final year a different person. This wasn't Kevin the failure but Kevin the success. He found the final-year work difficult – but then it is meant to be – and finally obtained an upper second class Honours degree. The laboratory in the States had offered him the opportunity of undertaking research for a PhD provided he got that upper second and, as we write, he is starting his research that, hopefully, will bring him huge success on the job market in years to come. Kevin is an excellent example of the powerful effect that work placements have on people and how it can change people's lives.

So, sometimes the 'career planning' happens by chance. The moral, if there is one, is not to dismiss avenues until they've been explored a little.

And finally ...

The important thing in all of this is to explore all options and encourage Chris to apply for anything that seems of interest. She may be in the fortunate position that a number of final year students find themselves in: they are offered a number of jobs and they have to choose the one that interests them most and which will see them reach their mid- and long-term goals more easily.

Also, be prepared for failure. Be prepared for Chris to submit six (or even sixty) applications and for none of them to bear fruit. It is a very competitive marketplace out there and employers can afford to be 'picky'. It's at this time that the 'arm around the shoulder' is needed most, even if it is a 'virtual arm' at the end of a telephone or computer.

Many graduates will start work in a job that is not ideally suited to their talents just to earn some money until the right opening becomes available. This is not a mistake. Working helps build a CV so that when the right job crops up Chris will be best placed to get it. Also, work tends to build both confidence and competence in reality as well as in the CV. Remind Chris that this may not be the job she dreamed of when she started out, but it could be in the right organisation.

Many organisations fill vacancies with internal trawls, i.e. they fill jobs from among the people they already employ, and she might later be in the right place at the right time to fill an internal vacancy that *is* her dream job.

Most graduates get their careers fixed up sooner or later. The difference between now and thirty years ago is that it probably takes just that little bit longer – so don't make comparisons with your own experience.

Explain the 'waiting game' to Chris and be there for her when she needs the support. It can be quite devastating to work for eight or more years getting a load of qualifications (GCSEs, A levels or Highers and a degree) to find that no one wants you. Someone, somewhere will want Chris and that's the message to convey.

The good news is that the graduate market seems to be expanding and there are now even more graduate opportunities. If you want more practical advice, check out *The Times top 100 graduate employers* (Birchall, 2005).

Supporting Chris in her steps as she leaves university and into the beyond is, of course, only the start of it. Our experience is that ex-students need support too… but that's another book!

Chapter 12

Other sources of information

There are many sources of information available and here we have tried to list the main ones relevant to you. Government agencies distribute information promoting policies and highlighting opportunities. Information applicable to all universities and students comes from the admissions system (UCAS) and the funding sources (Student Finance Direct). The quality of universities and their teaching is disseminated by TQI (Teaching Quality Information) and university performance indicators are available from HESA (Higher Education Statistics Agency).

The universities themselves promote their own courses through their prospectuses (write to 'The Registrar' asking for a current prospectus) and their websites (www.*NameOfUniversity*.ac.uk). Some university websites have areas specifically for parents.

When you look at all these sources remember that some will be providing factual information and others promoting themselves and their organisation.

Some of the sources are books and articles that will be available in your local library. University libraries are also often open to casual readers, though you will not be able to borrow books. Just tell the librarian that you are a parent of a prospective student and you are looking for information. Go armed with a list of things you want to find.

Official websites are more reliable than books because they will have been updated to deal with current government or university policy. If you do not have access at home then try your local library or get Chris to do it from school. There are always internet cafés if all else fails. Remember that the content of most websites can be saved to local memory (for example, a memory stick) so you can view them on any computer.

General information

Frameworks for Higher Education Qualifications, QAA
www.qaa.ac.uk/academicinfrastructure/FHEQ
These describe the achievement represented by Higher Education qualifications. There's one for England, Wales and Northern Ireland and a separate one for Scotland.

Higher Education Statistics Agency (HESA)
www.hesa.ac.uk
A central source for the collection and dissemination of statistics about publicly funded UK Higher Education. Data include, for example, the numbers of students studying within broad course areas.

Some information compares universities, but beware because prospective students (and their parents) are usually more concerned about the performance of the individual course rather than the institution.

National Union of Students
www.nusonline.co.uk
A range of practical and representational advice for students.

Quality Assurance Agency (QAA)
www.qaa.ac.uk
A government-funded agency that safeguards the public interest in the standards of Higher Education qualifications and encourages continuous improvement.

The QAA carries out and publishes reviews of individual universities and has reviewed individual subjects at universities, though the latter has been discontinued and the information may thus be out of date. The Frameworks for Higher Education Qualifications are also available from the QAA.

Stamford Test

www.ucas.com/stamford

An on-line test to broadly determine the degree subject a student might study.

Teaching Quality Information

www.tqi.ac.uk

Information about the quality of Higher Education at UK universities, including the results of the National Student Survey. This site is being built slowly and may not contain information for every course at every university, but where there is information, it is plentiful, and is to be read with caution!

Remember that the numbers of students answering the questions can be low and, of course, students have only answered the questions that they have been asked.

UCAS

www.ucas.com

The Universities and Colleges Admissions Service, which processes applications for courses at universities in the UK, but also provides general information, some of it aimed at parents.

Disabled students

Access to Learning

www.dfes.gov.uk/studentsupport/administrators/dsp_s ection_6.shtml

Conditions for eligibility for Access to Learning Funds.

Access to Learning Fund

www.direct.gov.uk/en/EducationAndLearning/Universit yAndHigherEducation/StudentFinance/FinanceForNew Students/DG_069884

General information.

Code of practice for the assurance of academic quality and standards in higher education. Section 3: students with disabilities, QAA (1999).
www.qaa.ac.uk/academicinfrastructure/codeOfPractice/ section3/COP_disab.pdf
Guidelines on how universities should help disabled students.

Disability Discrimination, Code of Practice for Further & Higher Education. Equality Commission for Northern Ireland, Belfast
www.equalityni.org/archive/pdf/DDisFHEAppCOP0106.pdf
A wide range of practical examples that might be used by universities to help students with disabilities.

Higher Education Statistics Agency. *Student tables: disability*
www.hesa.ac.uk/holisdocs/pubinfo/stud.htm
Tables showing the number and types of disabled students in the UK.

Skill: National Bureau for Students with Disabilities
www.skill.org.uk
National charity promoting opportunities for young people and adults with any kind of disability in post-16 education.

Special Educational Needs and Disability Act 2001, HMSO
www.opsi.gov.uk/acts/acts2001/20010010.htm
Legislation covering what universities might be expected to do for disabled students in the UK, except Northern Ireland.

The Disabled Students' Allowance
www.direct.gov.uk/en/DisabledPeople/EducationAndTr aining/HigherEducation/DG_10034898
Information on how to apply and what the allowance covers.

The Special Educational Needs and Disability (Northern Ireland) Order 2005, HMSO
www.opsi.gov.uk/si/si2005/20051117.htm
Legislation covering what universities might be expected to do for disabled students in Northern Ireland.

Jobs and careers

Birchall, M. (2005). *The Times top 100 graduate employers.*
High Fliers Publications Ltd, London.

Find a gap Ltd
www.findagap.com
Help with organising a gap year.

Find a student job
www.findastudentjob.com
Assistance and tips for getting a job while a student.

Gap-year.com
www.gap-year.com
Help with organising a gap year.

Graduate prospects
www.prospects.ac.uk
Claims to be "The UK's official graduate careers website." A mine of information on how to get a graduate job or embark on further study.

Milk-round
www.milkround.com
General and extensive advice on graduate careers.

Student finance

Student Finance Direct
www.studentsupportdirect.co.uk
A one-stop shop for all financial information (loans and fees), wherever you are in the UK.

Educational Grants Advisory Service
www.egas-online.org.uk
Guidance and advice on funding for those studying in post-16 education in the UK. Includes loans, grants, benefits, access funds, hardship funds, bursaries and charitable trusts.

Department for Children, Schools and Families
www.dfes.gov.uk/studentsupport
Official DCFS site for Higher Education student support. For students in England.

Student Finance Northern Ireland
www.studentfinanceni.co.uk
For students in Northern Ireland.

Student Finance Wales Contact Centre
www.studentfinancewales.co.uk
For students in Wales.

The Student Awards Agency for Scotland
www.saas.gov.uk
For students in Scotland.

UK Government. *Student Finance: what you could get*
www.direct.gov.uk/en/EducationAndLearning/UniversityAndHigherEducation/StudentFinance/FinanceForNew Students
Information on financial help for students in general, and in particular for those who are parents or have adult dependants, or have a low income.

Chapter 13

The jargon

No matter how much we tried, we could not write this book and accurately reflect what goes on in universities without slipping into jargon. In our case, jargon words are those that have a specialised meaning within education in general or in universities in particular. We have tried to define these as best we can below.

Access courses – designed to prepare students for Higher Education courses who do not have 'typical' entry qualifications for Higher Education. May be offered by further education colleges.

Bachelor's degree – usually the first degree a person will study for. Persons who complete this degree become Bachelors of Arts or Science or Engineering, etc., depending on the subject studied. Can be at Ordinary or Honours level (see later entries).

Certificate in/of Higher Education – awarded to students who have completed roughly a third of an Honours degree, i.e. one year's study.

Credits – scheme used by some universities to chart the accumulating knowledge and skills of students. The most common scheme awards 360 credits to a three-year Honours degree, i.e. 120 credits per year. Modules within this scheme typically attract between 5 and 40 credits, though 10 and 20 credit modules are usual.

Generally, one credit is the equivalent of 10 hours work; thus a 20 credit module equates to 200 'student effort hours'. This time includes all work associated with the module – attendance at classes, preparation of assessment work, extra reading, revision for examinations, etc.

Diploma in/of Higher Education – awarded to students who have completed roughly two thirds of an Honours degree, i.e. two years' study.

Foundation course – course designed to prepare students for a specific course of study at university. May be offered by further education colleges. Not to be confused with a Foundation degree.

Foundation degree – a vocational programme of study of variable duration, usually involving a period of work placement (perhaps with a student's own employer for 'day release' students), and which has been designed with employer input. At a level below that of an Honours degree.
On successful completion there is often the possibility of enrolling in the later stages of an Honours degree; this is called a 'top up'.

Graduate – a person who has been awarded a degree.

Hall of Residence – student accommodation, usually purpose built, usually university-owned and managed. Often has its own social space, bar, sports facilities, launderette, etc.

Higher Education – education and training of an advanced nature normally provided to students of 18 years of age and older, typically in universities. For a detailed description see the Quality Assurance Agency website *(www.qaa.ac.uk/academicinfrastructure/FHEQ).*

HNC and HND – Higher National Certificate and Higher National Diploma. Courses are usually in vocational subjects, last for approximately two years and are at a level below that of an Honours degree.

Honours degree – a programme of study, usually of three years' duration, that requires the study of additional material (usually in the form of modules) over that required for an Ordinary degree.

The Honours degree is the typical undergraduate (or first, or Bachelor's) degree, the degree most students are studying for. Includes a small element of investigative (research) work.

Master's degree – a programme of study of one or two years' duration that covers a narrow topic in greater depth and at a more advanced level than that of an Honours degree.

Module – a discrete course of study, containing its own assessment, within a degree programme. A single module may run across the whole academic year or be confined to terms or semesters.

In credit-based systems, credits are awarded for the successful completion of modules. Depending on the size of the modules, students typically study between three and twelve modules per year.

Ordinary degree – an undergraduate degree that is below Honours level. May be awarded to students who have not quite achieved Honours level, for example, who do not have sufficient credits for Honours level.

But beware, this is not always a sign of failure. In many subjects some Ordinary degrees are studied for in their own right – most Medicine degrees, for example, are Ordinary degrees.

Personal Development Plan (PDP) – a record, sometimes called a Progress File, kept by a student, of achievements and skills acquired at university or elsewhere, with plans for future development.

A good PDP will allow a student to chart his or her progress through university. The specific details vary from university to university, but all universities must offer PDPs to students.

Personal tutor – an individual, usually a member of academic staff, allocated to a student. The role of Personal Tutor varies enormously from university to university: some generally 'look after' their students, some consider academic or personal matters only, some both. Often a first port of call when a student encounters difficulty of any type.

PhD and DPhil – 'doctoral' degrees, Doctors of Philosophy. A programme of advanced study offered in most subjects (not just Philosophy), typically of three years' duration involving research into a narrow field.

Assessed by examination of a single document (a thesis) detailing the work done. The thesis usually makes an original contribution to knowledge. At a more advanced level than a Master's degree. Holders of PhDs and DPhils can use the title 'Dr'.

Postgraduate – a student, studying on a postgraduate course.

Postgraduate Certificate – awarded to students who have completed roughly a third of a Master's degree. This is not evidence of a failed Master's, but a legitimate outcome of a defined programme of study.

Postgraduate Course – courses at a higher level than an Honours degree, typically leading to a Postgraduate Certificate, Postgraduate Diploma, Master's degree, or PhD or DPhil.

Postgraduate Diploma – awarded to students who have completed roughly two thirds of a Master's degree. This is not evidence of a failed Master's, but a legitimate outcome of a defined programme of study.

Programme – what we have been calling a 'course' in this book, i.e. a programme of study leading to a university award, such as an Honours degree.

Prospectus – a booklet or website giving details of all courses, or a sub-set of courses, at a university or other institute of learning, aimed at potential applicants. Also typically contains details of other aspects of the institution such as accommodation, disability provision, sports, resources, etc.

Research Assessment Exercise (RAE) – a periodic assessment of the quality of research in universities. Universities that do well in research will often tell prospective students this, but beware: there may be no link between a university or a university department's RAE score and the ability of its staff to teach or 'look after' its students.

Semester – some universities divide the academic year into two teaching blocks called semesters. The first usually lasts from September/October to January/February and the second from then until May/June. Modules may be delivered on a semester basis.

Seminar – teaching method where a group of students and a lecturer meet to discuss aspects of the course in a less formal setting than that of a lecture.

Tariff – a points system used by UCAS for entry into Higher Education. Universities will make an offer to prospective students in terms of points, rather than on A level scores as was done in the past. Allows a wider range of entry qualifications to be considered by universities.

Term – universities usually teach 3 terms in a year, similar to school terms, though term lengths vary between universities. Modules may be arranged by terms or semesters.

Undergraduate – a student studying for a first or Bachelor's degree, such as an Honours degree.

Index